Measuring Housing Discrimination in a National Study

REPORT OF A WORKSHOP

Committee on National Statistics

Angela Williams Foster, Faith Mitchell, and Stephen E. Fienberg, Editors

Division of Behavioral and Social Sciences and Education

National Research Council

NATIONAL ACADEMY PRESS
Washington, DC

NATIONAL ACADEMY PRESS • 2101 Constitution Avenue, N.W. • Washington, DC 20418

The project that is the subject of this report was supported by contract SES-9709489 between the National Academy of Sciences and the Department of Housing and Urban Development. Any opinions, findings, conclusions, or recommendations expressed in this publication are those of the author(s) and do not necessarily reflect the views of the organizations or agencies that provided support for the project.

International Standard Book Number 0-309-08325-7

Additional copies of this report are available from National Academy Press, 2101 Constitution Avenue, N.W., Lockbox 285, Washington, DC 20055; (800) 624-6242 or (202) 334-3313 (in the Washington metropolitan area); Internet, http://www.nap.edu

Suggested Citation: National Research Council (2002) *Measuring Housing Discrimination in a National Study: Report of a Workshop.* Committee on National Statistics. Angela Williams Foster, Faith Mitchell, Stephen E. Fienberg, Editors. Division of Behavioral and Social Sciences and Education. Washington, DC: National Academy Press.

Printed in the United States of America

THE NATIONAL ACADEMIES

National Academy of Sciences
National Academy of Engineering
Institute of Medicine
National Research Council

The **National Academy of Sciences** is a private, nonprofit, self-perpetuating society of distinguished scholars engaged in scientific and engineering research, dedicated to the furtherance of science and technology and to their use for the general welfare. Upon the authority of the charter granted to it by the Congress in 1863, the Academy has a mandate that requires it to advise the federal government on scientific and technical matters. Dr. Bruce M. Alberts is president of the National Academy of Sciences.

The **National Academy of Engineering** was established in 1964, under the charter of the National Academy of Sciences, as a parallel organization of outstanding engineers. It is autonomous in its administration and in the selection of its members, sharing with the National Academy of Sciences the responsibility for advising the federal government. The National Academy of Engineering also sponsors engineering programs aimed at meeting national needs, encourages education and research, and recognizes the superior achievements of engineers. Dr. Wm. A. Wulf is president of the National Academy of Engineering.

The **Institute of Medicine** was established in 1970 by the National Academy of Sciences to secure the services of eminent members of appropriate professions in the examination of policy matters pertaining to the health of the public. The Institute acts under the responsibility given to the National Academy of Sciences by its congressional charter to be an adviser to the federal government and, upon its own initiative, to identify issues of medical care, research, and education. Dr. Kenneth I. Shine is president of the Institute of Medicine.

The **National Research Council** was organized by the National Academy of Sciences in 1916 to associate the broad community of science and technology with the Academy's purposes of furthering knowledge and advising the federal government. Functioning in accordance with general policies determined by the Academy, the Council has become the principal operating agency of both the National Academy of Sciences and the National Academy of Engineering in providing services to the government, the public, and the scientific and engineering communities. The Council is administered jointly by both Academies and the Institute of Medicine. Dr. Bruce M. Alberts and Dr. Wm. A. Wulf are chairman and vice chairman, respectively, of the National Research Council.

Preface

This report summarizes the main points made at a workshop held September 22-23, 2000, to review the design plan for a national study to measure discrimination in housing. The Committee on National Statistics of the National Research Council convened the workshop in response.to a request from the Office of Policy Development and Research of the Department of Housing and Urban Development (HUD). The workshop discussions encompassed a critique of the methods to be used for the national study, as well as the issues of how to define and measure discrimination. In addition to contributing to HUD's work, it is hoped that this report will advance thinking about methods for assessing discrimination, whether in housing or in other areas.

The workshop was chaired by Stephen E. Fienberg, Maurice Falk University Professor of Statistics and Social Science, Carnegie Mellon University, and overseen by a subcommittee of the Committee on National Statistics comprising Joseph Altonji, Department of Economics, Northwestern University; Roderick Little, School of Public Health, University of Michigan; and Charles Manski, Department of Economics, Northwestern University. The editors would like to thank the presenters for their contributions to the discussion. They include Joseph Altonji, Lawrence Bobo, Nancy Denton, Arthur Goldberger, Tom Jabine, Sanders Korenman, Tom Louis, Charles Manski, Susan Murphy, Steve Ross, Rob Santos, Gregory Squires, Margery Turner, and Min Zhou. In addition, George Galster participated in an earlier planning meeting that helped set the stage for the workshop. The editors also thank HUD for its sponsorship of the workshop, and for its patience in awaiting this final report. A full list of the workshop participants, with their affiliations, is provided in Appendix C.

This report has been reviewed in draft form by individuals chosen for their diverse perspectives and technical expertise, in accordance with procedures approved by the Report Review Committee of the National Research Council. The purpose of this independent review is to provide candid and critical comments that will assist the institution in making its published report as sound as possible and to ensure that the report meets institutional standards for objectivity, evidence, and responsiveness to the study charge. The review comments and draft manuscript remain confidential to protect the integrity of the deliberative process.

We thank the following individuals for their participation in the review of this report: Mary Frances Berry, Department of History, University of Pennsylvania, and chair, U.S. Commission on Civil Rights; Xavier de Souza Briggs, JFK School of Government, Harvard University; Alicia H. Munnell, Carroll School of Management, Boston College; William Rodgers, Department of Economics, College of William and Mary; and David R. Williams, Institute for Social Research, University of Michigan.

Although the reviewers listed above have provided many constructive comments and suggestions, they were not asked to endorse the conclusions or recommendations nor did they see the final draft of the report before its release. The review of this report was overseen by Eugene Hammel, Department of Demography, University of California at Berkeley. Appointed by the National Research Council, he was responsible for making certain that an independent examination of this report was carried out in accordance with institutional procedures and that all review comments were carefully considered. Responsibility for the final content of this report rests entirely with the authoring committee and the institution.

Angela Williams Foster, Faith Mitchell, and Stephen E. Fienberg, Editors

Contents

1

Introduction

Federal law prohibits housing discrimination on the basis of seven protected classes including race (see Box 1-1). Despite 30 years of legal prohibition under the Fair Housing Act, however, there is evidence of continuing discrimination in American housing, as documented by several recent reports (e.g., Massey and Lundy, 1998; Ondrich et al., 2000). In 1998, the Department of Housing and Urban Development (HUD) funded a $7.5 million independently conducted Housing Discrimination Survey (HDS) of racial and ethnic discrimination in housing rental, sales, and lending markets (Public Law 105-276). This survey is the third such effort sponsored by HUD. Its intent is to provide a detailed understanding of the patterns of discrimination in housing nationwide.

In 1999, the Committee on National Statistics (CNSTAT) of the National Research Council (NRC) was asked to review the research design and analysis plan for the 2000 HDS and to offer suggestions about appropriate sampling and analysis procedures. The review took the form of a workshop that addressed HUD's concerns about the adequacy of the sample design and analysis plan, as well as questions related to the measurement of various aspects of discrimination and issues that might bias the results obtained. The discussion also explored alternative methodologies and research needs. In addition to addressing methodological and substantive issues related specifically to the HDS, the workshop examined broader questions related to the measurement of discrimination. The workshop participants (listed in Appendix C) included representatives of

BOX 1-1 Overview of the Fair Housing Act

The 1968 Fair Housing Act prohibits discrimination in housing on the basis of five protected classes: race, color, religion, sex, and national origin. The act was amended in 1988 to expand the protected classes to include familial status and handicap. Individual jurisdictions may add to but may not subtract from the seven federally protected classes.

U.S. Code Title 42, Chapter 45, states the provisions of the Fair Housing Act. With the exception of exempted units, it is unlawful to engage in "discriminatory housing practices" in the sale or rental of a housing unit. The code outlines prohibited practices, which include refusing to sell or rent a unit and offering different terms or conditions on the basis of any protected class.

Section 3603 of the code allows for certain exemptions. One is for the lease or sale of a single-family house by the owner if that individual owns no more than three single-family houses. Additional provisions obtain, including that the house must be sold or rented without using a real estate agent or advertisement in violation of fair housing codes. Also exempted are units in living quarters occupied by the owner, provided no more than four families reside in the dwelling independently.

Section 3604 sets forth practices prohibited under the Fair Housing Act. Among these practices are the following:

- Refusing to sell or rent after a bona fide offer has been made
- Offering different terms, conditions, or privileges related to the unit
- Indicating preferences, limitations, or discrimination in advertisements
- Misrepresenting a unit's availability
- Refusing to permit a person with a disability to make "reasonable modifications" to the unit at the person's own expense

One or more of the seven protected classes cannot be a factor in the outcome of the housing transaction.

HUD and the Urban Institute (which is conducting the survey), as well as experts in the salient methodological and substantive areas. Formal recommendations were not developed because the discussion of these issues constituted the review required by HUD. This report provides a summary of the workshop discussions.

In addition to informing HUD's plans for the HDS, the workshop served as preparation for an upcoming NRC project on methods for assessing discrimination. This study will address broader methodological approaches for defining and measuring discrimination, incorporating what has been learned from the housing field and audit studies. It will examine the range of methods in current use and produce recommendations regarding those which most reliably differentiate discrimination from other differences. Both projects are part of a larger body of DBASSE reports on subjects related to the achievement of equal opportunity.[1]

THE HOUSING DISCRIMINATION SURVEY

The HDS is being conducted in three phases. The first phase, which began in 2000, involved an initial set of 20 metropolitan areas and as many as 6,000 matched-pair audits. The initial 20 sites allowed for over-time comparisons with the results of the earlier two surveys. An important aspect of the design is the determination of an "optimum" selection of an additional 40 sites to generate a valid national estimate of discrimination against specific minority groups (African Americans, Hispanics, Asians, and American Indians). As noted, the survey is being conducted by the Urban Institute, which also carried out the two previous discrimination surveys. A detailed description of the three phases of the HDS is provided in Chapter 2.

The HDS is using matched-pair audits to investigate housing discrimination, building on HUD's 20-year reliance on this methodology. In these

---

[1]*A Common Destiny: Blacks and American Society* (1989); *Measuring Poverty: A New Approach* (1995); *Title I Testing and Assessment: Challenging Standards for Disadvantaged Children* (1996); *Effects of Welfare on the Family and Reproductive Behavior* (1998); *Racial and Ethnic Differences in the Health of Older Americans* (1997); *Demographic and Economic Impacts of Immigration* (1997); *Health and Adjustment of Immigrant Children and Families* (1998); *Improving Schooling for Language-Minority Children* (1998); *Improving the Future of U.S. Cities Through Improved Metropolitan Area Governance* (1999); and *America Becoming: Racial Trends and Their Consequences* (2001).

audits, pairs of individuals are matched for "all" relevant characteristics other than those that are expected to lead to discrimination. If there are significant differences in the way members of the pairs are treated in the test setting, the matched-pair audit methodology attributes these differences to discrimination. The strengths and limitations of this approach are discussed in detail in Chapter 2.

HUD's goal is to develop statistically valid measures of the extent of racial and ethnic discrimination throughout a sample of American housing markets. The agency plans to use the results of the study to target future enforcement efforts more effectively, to direct legislative action needed to reduce discrimination, and to create "report cards" for the nation and for the communities studied that can be used to measure progress toward the goal of greater social integration.

KEY ISSUES DISCUSSED AT THE WORKSHOP

The major objective of the HDS is to measure the incidence of racial discrimination in the national housing market. The audit methodology and sampling frame applied to study discrimination against minorities in urban housing markets raise several key issues. The workshop discussions addressed these issues from both a methodological and substantive perspective.

Prior housing discrimination studies have focused on discrimination against African American and Hispanic households, whereas HDS 2000 extends the minority groups studied to include Asian Americans and American Indians. Consequently, an additional goal of the workshop was to address conceptual, methodological, and sociological issues related to measuring housing discrimination against these minority groups. Participants were also asked to address the application of the current audit methodology and sampling frame to studying subpopulations within the Asian community, as well as concentrations of American Indian groups in rural communities. Including these "underserved" populations raises additional measurement issues with regard to the study design, and the workshop discussions addressed these issues as well.[2]

Differential treatment of minority and white home seekers in a hous-

---

[2]Underserved populations or communities are those that have not previously been included in the HDS sampling frame, because of either their racial composition or their size.

ing market transaction does not necessarily mean that racial discrimination has occurred. The purpose of paired testing is to provide an objective means of determining whether differential treatment during a housing transaction is due to the race of the applicant. Since "all" household and housing unit factors other than race are controlled, racial discrimination is assumed to be the reason if differential treatment occurs.[3] This conclusion is based on the definition of racial discrimination as "the unequal treatment of equals on the basis of race" (Fix et al., 1993). The audit test also seeks to establish a realistic point of entry into the housing market and to control for various observable factors. Of course, the methodology does not control for all factors and is based on some untested assumptions. Housing market transactions, for example, involve both random and systematic factors. Characteristics or behaviors of the auditors or housing agents, among other factors, may affect the audit results. These random factors are not controlled for by the methodology and thus may not be observable by the audit researchers.

Past research addressing both systematic and random factors involved in housing transactions has led to the development of four measures of unequal or disparate treatment: (1) discriminatory inclination, (2) gross unfavorable treatment, (3) systematic unfavorable treatment, and (4) net market effects (Fix et al., 1993). The discussions at the workshop focused on two of these measures—gross unfavorable treatment and net market effect. Since these two measures mean different things depending on how the population of interest is defined, and since all estimates of housing discrimination are based on numerous audits, two other key issues were discussed: the appropriateness of weighting the audit results and the need for a clear definition of the population of interest.

HUD officials and researchers are currently weighting the results of audits performed on advertisements sampled from major metropolitan newspapers to obtain a more accurate estimate of discrimination in the housing market. Yet the appropriateness of this weighting scheme is contingent on the definition of the population of interest. The sampling frame may not reflect the entire housing market, but rather those housing units that are advertised in major metropolitan newspapers. This issue is most

---

[3]The characteristics controlled for include all legitimate reasons a minority applicant might receive treatment different from that of a majority or white applicant, as well as other illegitimate or illegal reasons for denial (such as familial status).

salient when one considers that majority and minority home seekers may face a dual housing market; the sources used for seeking a housing unit may also differ by race. The design of the sampling frame should ideally reflect these differences.

REPORT ORGANIZATION

The workshop was organized into three sessions addressing the following topics: (1) the purpose of and key policy and methodological issues related to the HDS, (2) preparations for Phase II of the HDS audit— auditing of discrimination in underserved urban communities and implications of the preceding methodological discussion for the Phase II design plan, and (3) the HUD and other methodologies for measuring discrimination. This report is structured to reflect the key issues raised on each of these topics and their relevance to the objectives of the workshop.

Chapter 2 presents an overview of the 2000 HDS, including its objectives and design. This chapter also reviews the testing methodology, with emphasis on its application to the detection of housing discrimination. Included is a summary of the workshop discussion on the advantages and disadvantages of paired testing, as well as methodological concerns regarding its use to identify discrimination in housing markets. Chapter 3 summarizes the workshop discussion on clearly defining or identifying the population of interest, in particular on whether the current HDS sampling methodology and study design do, in fact, capture the population about which inferences are drawn by researchers. Chapter 4 presents highlights of the discussion on defining housing discrimination and on the important distinction between disparate impact discrimination and disparate treatment discrimination. Chapter 5 summarizes the discussion of how to model and define housing discrimination. Finally, Chapter 6 addresses special concerns related to applying the audit study design to underserved populations, particularly Asian Americans and American Indians and those living in small metropolitan areas. In addition, three appendices are provided: Appendix A is a paper prepared for the workshop that gives a detailed description of the HDS; Appendix B is a second paper addressing some methodological issues associated with the HDS audit in a framework that is in some ways richer than that which has spawned the paired-testing methodology; and Appendix C contains the workshop agenda and a list of the workshop participants.

2

Overview of the 2000 Housing Discrimination Study

The HDS, announced by HUD Secretary Andrew Cuomo in November 1998, is intended to be a 3-year study of discrimination in the U.S. housing market. The results will extend and expand HUD's 20-year history of measuring discrimination in housing through the methodology of paired testing or audits.

STUDY OBJECTIVES

The principal objective of the HDS is to develop a national estimate of discrimination in housing, as well as metropolitan-level estimates that can be compared across time. As noted earlier, report cards will be developed at both the national and community levels to provide a benchmark against which to measure progress toward eliminating discrimination. The study will explore the statistical concept of racial discrimination, which may or may not be the same as the legal concept. The law determines discrimination in individual cases of real people; the HDS audit seeks to create a measure of discrimination by which the incidences of discrimination can be counted.

While past HDS audits have measured some effects of discrimination for particular cities, the current audit will expand that effort and obtain more detail on where discrimination occurs within a city. Further, the study will assess what kinds of housing markets may have an effect on racially disparate treatment. The HDS audit has clear implications for enforcing fair housing laws. Because the study is an audit, however, no enforcement activity will occur as a direct result of the testing outcomes.

STUDY DESIGN

As noted in Chapter 1, the 2000 HDS audit involves 60 sites and is a multiphase study: Phase I, including 20 sites, began in 2000; Phase II began in 2001; and Phase III will begin in 2002. In Phase I, an attempt is being made to obtain national estimates of disparate treatment in home seeking among African American and Hispanic groups; these estimates will be used to measure changes in discrimination over time since the most recent HDS audit (1989), as well as for future studies. To assess the appropriateness of the current testing methodology for other ethnic groups, the Phase I study also includes pilot testing for Asian American and American Indian groups. Phases II and III, which were still in the development stages when the workshop was convened, are intended to expand upon Phase I by producing more-precise estimates of the incidence of discrimination at the national level. Based on the results of pilot testing in Phase I, Phase II will extend the analysis of minority groups from African Americans and Hispanics to Asian Americans and American Indians. The study will include site-specific estimates and pilot sites for three Asian American groups— Chinese, Korean, and Southeast Asian—and for American Indian groups in rural areas.

Estimation of discrimination for these populations represents a new area for the HDS. Measurement issues arise with each new group being studied. For example, measuring discrimination in the American Indian community requires changes to the original sampling design. Rather than focusing in metropolitan areas, the sampling frame will include less-populated areas in an attempt to depict more accurately the housing market these groups face.

PHASE I STRATIFIED RANDOM SAMPLING DESIGN

The Phase I design uses two-stage cluster sampling. The sampling frame is a collection of 105 metropolitan statistical areas satisfying the following criteria: (1) according to 1980 census data, the population exceeded 100,000 residents; and (2) the concentration of African American households exceeded a nominal threshold. Metropolitan areas were stratified into (1) those sites for which both African American and Hispanic testing would occur because the population and concentration thresholds were exceeded for both ethnic groups; and (2) those sites for which only African American testing would occur because the thresholds were met only for that population.

The first stage of the sampling frame, area probability sampling, involves selecting sites for the African American and Hispanic samples, with selection probabilities proportional to population size (using census data). The second stage entails selecting advertisements for both rental and sales housing from the Sunday newspapers within those metropolitan areas. Prior to sampling, analysts identify the major metropolitan newspaper for every site on the basis of circulation and geographic coverage. In the case of sites with more than one major newspaper circulating to different communities within the metropolitan area, the newspapers are rotated from week to week. This rotation is employed in an attempt to capture potential differences in patterns of advertisement across the different communities. If such differences exist, the sampling frame results in better coverage of the entire geographic area.

PAIRED-TESTING METHODOLOGY

As noted in Chapter 1, the 2000 HDS employs the paired-testing methodology used in prior HDS audits. The study includes approximately 5,000 tests from a sample of about 20,000 newspaper advertisements of available renter- and owner-occupied housing units.

Paired testing has been used extensively in studies on employment, homeowner's insurance, mortgage lending, and automobile sales. Its most extensive use, however, is in the area of housing, both renter- and owner-occupied, in which there have been three national studies (including the current HDS). Paired testing has also been used in multiple small regional studies and in a great deal of enforcement testing, where it has led to numerous fair housing cases and settlements.

The protocol for a paired test in housing studies is designed to establish a point of entry into the housing market that is realistic and consistent for all testers. In paired testing, two people (auditors) pose as equally qualified customers inquiring about an advertised housing unit. The only apparent difference between the two auditors is their race or ethnicity; they are similar in age, gender, dress, and other observable characteristics that can be controlled a priori. The testing coordinator is responsible for sending audit pairs to a test site, determining their assigned characteristics, and ensuring that they match on all observable characteristics except race. The auditors are trained to follow a common protocol when they engage in the housing market transaction to minimize the effect of naturally occurring personal differences. Since characteristics other than race that might distinguish the testers and possibly influence the housing agent have been controlled for, differences in auditor reports are assumed to be attributable to racial differences in treatment.

There are a number of advantages to using paired testing instead of market data. One advantage is that the testing provides a structured point of entry that yields an endogenous sample and protocol. Once a point of entry has been established and a sample drawn, that sample represents an exogenous entry into the market or is an exogenous sample of entries into the market.

A second advantage of paired testing relates to mitigating behavior of individuals. Economic theory suggests that people act to maximize their welfare. A limitation of market data is that they cannot measure whether individuals anticipate that they will be discriminated against and take mitigating actions to limit the effect of that discrimination. For example, an individual may pursue a higher-cost lender because he expects to face discrimination in the prime mortgage market. Mortgage lending data (market data) will show that this person applied for a mortgage and was approved for the loan. However, the data will not reflect racial differences in underwriting or the higher premium the individual paid for the loan. Housing segregation is another area that may reflect mitigating behavior. A family may visit a particular real estate agency because they expect to be treated fairly. If, however, that agency focuses on housing that happens to be located in minority communities, the agency's sales will result in racial residential segregation. When analyzing market data, one often cannot control for the cost of such mitigating behavior. Paired testing is therefore preferred because it does not count this potentially costly behavior.

By exploiting the benefits of paired testing, the 2000 HDS can provide estimates of housing discrimination that are not obtainable using housing market data. The methodology employed in the HDS audit uses a common protocol. By assigning characteristics and controlling for the behavior of the auditors, the researchers attempt to ensure the objectivity of the study and limit the influence of mitigating factors. If a minority tester's expectation about being discriminated against affected his or her behavior in the test, the analysts would observe differences in behavior across the minority testers. Therefore, one measure of mitigating behavior is deviation from the protocol, observed through heterogeneous outcomes of tester pairs.

Housing market data and paired testing are ideally complementary, with testing capturing the level and frequency of discrimination while ignoring the potential effect of mitigating behavior. Market data will capture mitigating behavior, but may miss some of the substantial costs associated with that behavior. Unable to measure whether observed outcomes result from perceived discrimination or racial preferences, market data may understate the effects of discrimination. Conversely, testing data may overstate the effects of discrimination in a particular housing market. Thus, for example, African American auditors may be discriminated against more often than African American home seekers in the housing market because testing does not allow for mitigating behavior.

During his comments, Stephen Ross, Department of Economics, University of Connecticut, suggested that paired testing can clearly distinguish between disparate treatment and disparate impact discrimination and other possible biases that may exist in market data. Market data may also capture variation across practices of housing agents resulting in racial differences in outcomes. Testing avoids this variation by sending auditors to the same housing agent and thus provides a clean test for one type of discrimination. Paired testing also avoids omitted variable bias, endogeneity, and sample selection bias (Ross, 2000). It provides a controlled environment that assigns or controls for many characteristics of the auditor and collects data on unassigned attributes of the auditor and housing unit. Extensive training and protocols diminish the effect of these potentially biasing components.

Testing has already proven to be effective in the enforcement arena, possibly resulting in more-comprehensive settlements. Some social science researchers have also used testing to identify the underlying dynamics of discrimination in ways previously unavailable. Although there are practical and theoretical limitations to audit tests, it is important to note the usefulness of the tool and the advantages to further developing audit methodology. Improvements to the current audit methodology discussed during the workshop included performing more tests within a site, making the audit process more standardized, and using actual home seekers instead of trained auditors.

PAIRED TESTING AND THE 2000 HDS

The use of paired testing in the 2000 HDS begins with the researchers sending the selected newspaper advertisements to the local test coordinator, who makes advance calls to verify the availability and eligibility of the advertised unit. Workshop participants asked about the criteria used to determine which audit pair will visit a particular advertised unit. Urban Institute researchers responded that advertisements from each metropolitan newspaper are randomized and assigned a control number from 1 to N. The local test coordinator receives a faxed copy of the advertisement and begins with control no. 1, proceeding in sequential order until the required number of tests for that week has been performed. After verifying the unit's availability, the test coordinator completes a test assignment form that standardizes the profiles of the two auditors. The form also randomizes the order in which the auditors visit the housing unit and provides a complete financial and household profile to ensure the credibility of the auditor as an applicant for housing.

The auditors then have a face-to-face meeting with the housing agent. They inquire about the specific advertised unit, as well as other housing that may be available. In both sales and rental cases, the auditors inspect the housing unit. After departing from the site, each auditor immediately completes a series of standard forms that captures the testing experience. The test forms are used to record various objective factors, including waiting time, name of the agent, documents received, documentation required, amenities of the unit, and other factors related to unit cost. For sales testing, the forms include information on whether the tester was asked about loan prequalification or the process involved in securing a mortgage.

From the forms, researchers obtain characteristics of the homes that were inspected, along with addresses of additional units recommended by the agent. For a percentage of cases, a narrative of the entire visit is also provided and reviewed during debriefing. The test coordinator compiles all materials related to the test and sends them to the Urban Institute for data entry. The local test coordinator performs no treatment comparisons; only members of the HDS audit research team make an assessment of racially disparate treatment.

As noted, Phase I includes 20 sites; among them are African American/white sites, Hispanic/white sites, Asian American/white sites, and American Indian sites. Overall there are approximately 1,200 paired rental tests and 1,200 paired sales tests. The current Phase I design does not include non-white testers paired with other non-white testers (e.g., African American/Hispanic or African American/Asian American pairs); these pairings may be considered in Phase II. Participant Stephen Fienberg, Maurice Falk University Professor of Statistics and Social Science and Acting Director, Center for Automated Learning and Discovery, Carnegie Mellon University, noted that non-white/non-white testing could bolster what is learned from white/non-white comparisons.

Fienberg expressed concern about the fact that those conducting the HDS are involved in both measurement and enforcement activities. That linkage could have implications for the ongoing nature of the study and the validity of the data collected, especially if it is in the minds of the parties being tested. The HDS audits are not the only testing occurring in the test sites. HUD has funded testing for many years, and all of the agents included in the HDS results are operating in markets where there is also a fair-housing group performing enforcement testing. Housing providers are aware that testing is ongoing; therefore the confidentiality of the HDS audits is an issue. Perhaps advance word of the HDS could spread and distort the results. If real estate agents suspect they have been audited, they may contact other members of the agent community within a test site, thus invalidating the remaining audits. The researchers responded that they believe they would learn quickly if housing agents were aware of nonroutine testing efforts.[1]

Of methodological concern is whether researchers discard an audit when a housing provider identifies a member of the audit pair as an auditor. The researchers responded that auditors are trained to address issues of detection and to continue with the test when possible. In some instances, the test coordinator may decide to invalidate a test. Detection occurred in another study in a manner that would have compromised subsequent audits at a site, and testing in that site was terminated. Researchers have not encountered this problem in the HDS to date.

---

[1]Researchers stated they believe they would be able to learn whether housing agents suspected a systemic audit because those performing field reconnaissance and local fair housing agencies would be made aware of this information.

CHANGES IN THE NATURE OF HOUSING DISCRIMINATION AND IMPLICATIONS FOR THE AUDIT DESIGN

One participant expressed concern that the paired-testing methodology generally focuses on racially differential treatment at the pre-application stage of housing market transactions. Yet testing and enforcement data from some fair housing agencies suggest that minority home seekers are also vulnerable to discrimination in the form of different terms and conditions after their application has been submitted for review. Consequently, audit results will yield an estimate of discrimination for a portion of housing market transactions, but may not provide the benchmark that HUD desires—changes in the nature of discrimination over time. The number of incidents of discrimination may decline not because discrimination has decreased, but because it has shifted to another stage of the housing transaction. If this is the case, the current audit protocol will underestimate racial discrimination.

Representatives from HUD and the Urban Institute acknowledged that the nature of housing discrimination may be changing. The question they face is how to measure post-application discrimination, since auditors do not submit applications. While auditors involved in sales testing make multiple visits in order to appear as serious buyers and to view multiple properties, they do not make offers on any of the units they see. The paired-testing methodology is probably not the solution for addressing this issue, and the researchers asked for suggestions for alternative methods that could be used to capture this phenomenon.

It was also noted that in many housing markets, real estate agents are now asking individuals to sign up with a buyer's broker before viewing any housing units. This practice poses an additional challenge for the audit structure. First, since auditors may be involved in multiple tests, the practice can increase the likelihood of their being detected. Also, researchers believe the influence of the buyer's broker is more important in some housing markets than in others. Through auditor reports, they collect information on whether minority auditors are required to sign such an agreement while white auditors are not. Racial differences in these requirements may represent discrimination.

3

Defining the Population of Interest

A significant portion of the workshop discussion focused on identifying a probabilistic econometric model for identifying the population of interest consistent with HUD's objectives. Participants suggested that before assessing whether the current model is appropriate for the parameters of interest, some important questions need to be addressed:

- What is the model for the outcomes?
- What is actually being sampled?
- Given the sample, what is the role of sampling weights? How does the analysis move from paired events to a universe of populations?
- What is the population to which one can generalize from such events?
- How does that universe relate to the housing market?

TARGET POPULATION

During the workshop, the sponsors defined the target population as the housing market in the test sites. Participants noted that the target population differs from the population suggested by the sampling frame, and posed the question, What is the correct definition for the population given the sampling frame? The researchers responded that the actual population is the housing stock served by advertisements appearing in a site's major metropolitan newspaper on Sunday.

Participants suggested an alternative sampling frame that would resemble the target population more closely. This sample would include all known newspapers with housing advertisements circulating in the test site. With this method, researchers would lose a priori knowledge of the selection probability for a given advertisement. However, this limited knowledge may not be necessary since the true probabilities can be computed and weighted appropriately. This alternative sampling frame would yield unequal probabilities of selection, but participants did not view this as a major limitation.

Another alternative, raised by Tom Louis of the RAND Corporation, would be to abandon the sample survey goal in favor of an alternative unbiased selection procedure. The objective would be to select neighborhoods or communities in which advertising is prevalent without the goal of selecting a random sample. This method would ignore the sampling procedure and would not be concerned with sample survey weights or statistical comparisons within samples. Louis also noted that the reliance on advertisements produces selection bias since part of the market is missed (e.g., availability that is "advertised" through word of mouth). The researchers responded that pilot tests in the current study design include nonadvertisement sampling that begins to address this issue by identifying areas that are either protected (e.g., gated communities) or neglected (e.g., small communities that do not typically advertise available housing units in newspapers). Field reconnaissance in these areas provides researchers with available housing stock from which a secondary sample is drawn.

Participants discussed several ways to make the sampling frame more realistic. For example, one could look at the income and asset distribution of the minority population in individual metropolitan areas and sample housing units on the basis of that distribution. Urban Institute researchers pointed out that this sampling frame is quite different from one in which the sample of units is based on the distribution of where minorities currently live—an alternative approach offered during the discussion of auditing in underserved communities (see Chapter 6). The researchers expressed concern about this latter modification because it would institutionalize outcomes that may be the result of discrimination.

Participants were asked to discuss ways of making the sample more representative of the target populations, but in a neutral manner with respect to potential variants existing in the housing market. There was substantial agreement that this would be extremely difficult to do unless HUD were able to clarify the population to which it wants to generalize. The alternatives to the sampling frame discussed by participants included some that represent an attempt to overcome the limitations of the paired-testing methodology and allow alternative forms of generalization. Participants agreed that the current methodology poses many difficulties when applied to underserved communities, in which the paradigm does not appear to work well given differences in housing market structures. For example, it is highly unlikely a white individual would seek housing in some small, predominantly minority community.

POTENTIAL BIAS IN TEST SITE SELECTION

Workshop participants noted that many larger metropolitan areas have newspapers targeted to particular ethnic communities. The housing search patterns for people in some communities, especially minority groups, may not include advertisements in the major Sunday newspaper. In such cases, the initial sampling frame would not encompass advertisements more likely to be read by the subpopulation of interest, a limitation that would have implications for the credibility of the point of entry into the housing market that the researchers were trying to establish. Furthermore, omitting certain newspapers from the sampling frame could compromise the ability to draw inferences about the population the auditors represent.

The researchers noted that the sampling frame will be modified during the pilot phase of the study to include alternative advertisement sources, such as small neighborhood papers. For five specific sites, two types of enhancements to the usual newspaper advertisement sample are being used.

The first type of enhancement involves exploring the overall distribution of newspaper advertisements independently for rentals and sales, with the audit researchers looking at the relative distribution of those advertisements across neighborhoods within an audit site. Researchers will assess the multisource enhancements used in the pilot studies and develop a sampling frame for selecting advertisements in Phase II of the study. In Phase II, researchers will draw from a multiframe sampling source, using multiple neighborhood or community newspapers. However, sampling issues arise from multiple newspaper advertisement sources. In particular, the sponsors asked the workshop participants to discuss the implications for the sampling frame of the potential overlap in housing units—units that are sampled more than once because they are advertised in several papers.

Some participants questioned why multiple newspaper sources were not included in the Phase I study. The researchers responded that they wished to preserve known probabilities of selection for the advertisements. Devising a method to calculate the sampling probabilities would have been daunting given multiple newspapers and the fact that on a given day, advertisements must be drawn from 22 sites. In addition, the researchers wanted to mirror the 1989 sampling procedure. They acknowledged the limitations of this method.

Researchers noted further that the Phase I sampling frame was chosen to be comparable with the 1989 HDS. The newspaper methodology used for the 1989 and 2000 HDS to select advertised housing units does not reach the entire housing market. In fact, many minorities often do not seek housing opportunities in areas that do not receive a large amount of newspaper coverage. In addition, there are issues within minority neighborhoods and other types of areas regarding obtaining access to the housing stock that is available for both rental and sales. In some instances, it is unlikely a majority individual would seek housing in certain minority neighborhoods. In other instances, housing units may not be advertised in mainstream or community neighborhoods. Participants also discussed issues involved in testing in smaller metropolitan areas, some of which are joint rural-type counties.

The second enhancement of the sample involves obtaining census estimates for the proportion of available rental and sales housing for each test site. During the initial visit, auditors will ask the housing agent for the addresses of similar units. The resulting information will yield an auxiliary set of addresses to be used in identifying underrepresented areas that never reach the major metropolitan newspapers. Census housing market data will be matched with the auxiliary addresses. The researchers will then sample from these underrepresented areas—areas with fewer advertisements than available housing units—which are likely to be in minority communities.

DRAWING INFERENCES TO THE POPULATION OF INTEREST

In assigning tester characteristics, researchers guarantee that auditors are qualified for the housing units. Workshop participants suggested that by allowing for individuals who are on the margin financially, analysts may miss the discrimination of interest. Specifically, some participants believe that pairs of clearly qualified and clearly unqualified home seekers of differing races would receive similar treatment (either acceptance or rejection), but that on the margin, housing agents would make more subjective judgments and exercise greater discretion by offering additional assistance or compensation to the nonminority tester. By representing only eminently qualified testers, therefore, the audit results may understate the real degree of housing discrimination in the market. The sponsors responded that they believe discrimination may occur for both marginal and overqualified individuals and that both forms of discrimination are important to measure. The strategy of the study, however, is to identify clear and convincing disparate treatment when less discretion on the part of housing agents is allowed.

Participants discussed whether the population from which the auditors are drawn is a fair representation of the people who are seeking housing, in other words, whether the audit findings can be used to generalize about the discrimination a typical couple would face in the housing market. Participants suggested that unobservable characteristics of the testers may represent differences from the population of home seekers and that these characteristics may not be eliminated through training or protocols. However, as Stephen Ross noted, audit pairs conduct more than one audit. Since many of the pairs are fixed in terms of the people who make them up, their experiences in different settings allow researchers to test for whether unobservable tester characteristics matter. This issue is discussed further in Chapter 5.

Ross noted that the researchers have a difficult problem in dealing with very small sample sizes. HUD wants not only a national measure of housing discrimination and changes in the national incidence of discrimination, but also individual metropolitan measures. The audit methodology will produce only 70 samples. Accordingly, the research team will explore different options for obtaining exact estimates, such as permutation-type estimators or estimators that are corrected for small sample sizes. Such methods were not discussed during the workshop, but Ross (2000) notes that because permutation tests rely on frequency data, weights cannot be used.

WEIGHTING ADVERTISED UNITS

Participants noted it may be impractical to sample every newspaper in a large metropolitan area, but, as noted earlier, researchers are exploring the use of multiple papers and other advertisement resources in smaller areas, where a multiframe sampling source is more practical. The Urban Institute can use data gathered on the relationship between the sample and the population for these smaller areas to provide information about potential differences in the incidence of discrimination across advertisement sources.

Some participants were unclear on the appropriate weight that should be applied to the results, but noted that it should reflect the universe of available housing stock. Weighting audit results by housing unit size may not be particularly relevant, but weights should incorporate the various sources of information on housing availability, including major metropolitan newspapers, community newspapers, Internet-related databases, the Realtors® database (or MultiList), and other sources. Participants discussed the implications of accessing a fairly comprehensive database for available sales housing, such as the MultiList available to real estate agents. Perhaps such a list would serve as a base against which researchers could sample units and create approximate weights. Although participants did not know of the feasibility of this option, one stated it is more appropriate to obtain approximate weights for the right population than precise equal probability weights for the wrong population. Each specification has associated trade-offs that should be considered before results are reported.

4

Defining Housing Discrimination

The goal of the HDS is to measure the incidence of disparate treatment discrimination by housing agents during their interaction with borrowers who approach them as a result of a newspaper advertisement. Adverse disparate treatment could result from racial prejudice, financial incentives of the real estate agent, or other factors. The goal of the study is not to determine the cause of racial differences in treatment.

Stephen Fienberg commented that studies of discrimination in labor markets (e.g., Heckman, 1998) address the notion of distinguishing between market discrimination and the discrimination encountered by a random person responding to a randomly selected advertisement. The methodology in the labor market context is similar to that employed in the HDS audit. Heckman's paper offers the following definition of discrimination: "an otherwise identical person is treated differently by virtue of that person's race or gender, and race and gender by themselves have no direct effect on productivity." According to Heckman, discrimination is the effect of race that arises from a *ceteris paribus* hypothetical experiment in which race is allowed to vary while all other aspects of the individual and circumstances are held constant.

DISPARATE TREATMENT VERSUS DISPARATE IMPACT

During the discussion of methodological implications of the Phase II audit design, participants explored the differences between disparate treatment and disparate impact discrimination. Disparate treatment discrimination is defined as negative treatment of minority candidates due solely to the candidates' race. Disparate impact discrimination occurs when a system is put in place that is not discriminatory in intent, but negatively impacts a particular group of individuals. When housing providers deny or make housing unavailable to persons on the basis of characteristics not protected by the Fair Housing Act and when these characteristics are correlated with race, the result is disparate impact discrimination, not disparate treatment discrimination.

Disparate impact would occur, for example, if a lending institution did not finance older homes. In this case, the basis for denial would not be one of the classes protected by fair housing laws, and the policy would be universally applied. If racial minorities are much more likely to live in older homes than whites, however, the policy would exclude a higher proportion of racial minorities. Although whites and minorities would be *treated* similarly, the policy would adversely impact the protected group and thus constitute a form of discrimination. The housing provider would have to demonstrate that there was a business necessity for the policy and establish that there was no less discriminatory alternative that could serve the same business objective. Audit methodology is designed to measure only disparate treatment discrimination.

During his presentation, Gregory Squires, Department of Sociology, The George Washington University, suggested that, contrary to what some believe, paired testing can potentially uncover the existence of disparate impact discrimination in a given housing market. He asserted that, based on information provided to the minority and white auditors during the test, analysts can observe instances of disparate impact not recorded as disparate treatment. For example, the housing provider might share with the auditor information about the agency's policies and practices that may differ for minority and white home seekers. This information would not necessarily appear on the auditor's forms, but would be part of the narrative the auditor provided to the researchers. Though the policies highlighted would be applied to both minority and white auditors, they could differentially impact minority home seekers.

A related discussion addressed the ability to measure discrimination statistically given the legal definition. Some individual and household characteristics that are associated with disparate effects have a disparate impact because their distributions vary with race. As noted earlier, for enforcement audits, testing coordinators control for other factors to isolate the effect of race on the treatment recorded. Participants questioned the experimental approach used in enforcement audits and employed in the HDS. While conceptually one can hold all factors but race constant, doing so may not be possible in the actual housing market. In contrast with an experiment where a patient is given a placebo or treatment, one cannot assign or change an individual's racial identity. In the absence of this ability to randomize, researchers typically use an "approximate" study design that cannot be manipulated experimentally.

Participants noted that the methodology used is dependent on the research question of interest. Some participants expressed the underlying question as: If African Americans were whites or whites were African Americans, how would they be treated in the housing market? This question suggests a baseline of no racial discrimination. Other participants argued for a different framing of the question: In the absence of racial discrimination, how would a minority or majority home seeker be treated during the housing transaction?

GROSS AND NET ADVERSE TREATMENT

As discussed by Ross in his workshop remarks and his paper "Paired Testing and the 2000 Housing Discrimination Study" (see Appendix A), the HDS data are used to generate two common alternative measures of differential treatment. The first, *gross adverse treatment*, measures the frequency of audits in which a white auditor was treated favorably and a minority auditor was treated unfavorably. The second measure of differential treatment, *net adverse treatment*, measures the frequency with which the white auditor was treated favorably, minus the frequency with which the minority tester was treated favorably. Differential treatment could result from discrimination by the housing agent or from legitimate, not discriminatory factors. The gross measure will count legitimate nondiscriminatory racial differences (e.g., the unit having actually been rented between the visits of the white and minority auditors) as instances of adverse treatment because researchers cannot observe the intent of the housing agent. While these instances will be counted in the net measure as well, the presumption is that if differential treatment is not due to race and the order of audit visits is randomized by race, rates of adverse treatment for whites and minorities will cancel each other out.

The gross measure of adverse treatment, then, overestimates discrimination by including nondiscriminatory disparate treatment resulting from random, unobserved differences in auditors. Conversely, the net measure, although intended to capture differences in treatment that result from racial discrimination, underestimates discrimination. The hypothesis underlying the net measure is that the frequency with which the minority auditor is treated adversely because of factors unrelated to race can be proxied by the frequency with which the white auditor is treated adversely. Underestimates of discrimination result because instances in which the white auditor is treated less favorably are netted out, even though these differences may be attributable to unobserved adverse treatment of the minority auditor (Ondrich et al., 2000). The use of gross and net measures is discussed in greater detail in Chapter 5.

5

Developing a Model of
Housing Discrimination

CORE TREATMENT VARIABLES

HDS 2000 is collecting data on core treatment variables with which analysts will measure change since the 1989 study (see Table 5-1). These variables include measures of terms and conditions, housing availability, and general sales effort on the part of the agent. Data on additional treatment variables collected from the sales audits are intended to capture changes in the housing market. These variables provide objective measures of how the auditor was treated during the housing transaction and are used to measure racially disparate treatment during the audit.

HDS 2000 also includes new variables, not measured previously, regarding financing assistance offered by the agent. This addition is intended to capture a shift in the housing market whereby real estate agents appear to be playing a much greater role in providing borrowers with mortgage information. Many agents prequalify borrowers for the type and amount of mortgage they can receive instead of referring the applicant to a lending institution. Since this process is completed before the agent shows the potential buyers available housing that meets their needs or desires, it provides increased opportunity for racially disparate treatment.

USE OF GROSS AND NET MEASURES

In the discussion of the HDS model, Arthur Goldberger, Department of Economics, University of Wisconsin, suggested a modification of the

TABLE 5-1 Core Treatment Variables

Rental Only	Rental and Sales	Sales Only
Terms and Conditions	Housing Availability	Financing Assistance
• Application fee required • Special rental incentives offered • Rent includes extra amenities	• Access denied: no appointment or no unit available • Advertised unit available • Units similar to advertised unit available	• Assistance with financing volunteered • Auditor told he/she is not qualified • Auditor told fixed-rate conventional financing available • Auditor told adjustable-rate conventional financing available
	Sales Effort	Sales Effort
	• Questions asked about income • Questions asked about reasons for need to move • Invitation to call back	• Follow-up phone call

NOTE: This is not an exhaustive list of core treatment variables in the 2000 HDS. SOURCE: The variables in the table are those collected in both the 1989 HDS audit and the 2000 HDS audit.

model. When looking at population data rather than experimental data, researchers are interested in observing the frequency of adverse treatment for minorities in the housing market. The researchers proxy this quantity with a Bernoulli variable, Y_{it}, that measures adverse treatment for minority and white auditors for auditor race i and test t:

$$Y_{it} = \begin{cases} 1 & \text{if the individual was treated favorably} \\ 0 & \text{if the individual was treated unfavorably} \end{cases}$$

The race-specific average of Y_{it} gives the proportion of tests, for each race, in which auditors were treated favorably.

The gross measure of discrimination is the proportion of tests in which the minority auditor was treated unfavorably and the white auditor was treated favorably, P_{10}. The net measure of discrimination is the difference between the gross measure (P_{10}) and the proportion of tests in which the white auditor was treated unfavorably compared with the minority auditor, P_{01} (i.e., net measure = $P_{10} - P_{01}$) (see also Chapter 4.) P_{01} is a proxy for the frequency of adverse treatment incidences against minorities that are unrelated to race. P_{01} may be a poor proxy, however, if it includes deliberate reverse discrimination, which is subtracted out of the net measure.

The discussion frequently returned to the need to clearly define the concept of discrimination. To find the correct measure of discrimination, participants contemplated a conceptual experiment in which auditors are matched perfectly on all observable characteristics and encounter completely identical circumstances during their visit to a housing agent. Under these circumstances, the researchers believe the correct measure of the incidence of disparate treatment discrimination is the gross measure. One could measure both reverse racial discrimination (P_{01}) and racial discrimination (P_{10}), although the latter is the quantity of interest. The Urban Institute researchers noted, however, that this conceptual experiment is unachievable.

Additional discussion centered on the standard for housing market transactions, more specifically, the solutions for the joint probabilities in Table 5-2 in the absence of housing discrimination. Workshop participants suggested that the Urban Institute should consider the solutions for P_{ij} and their implications for the net and gross measures of adverse treatment. These solutions for varying levels of housing discrimination would help the Urban Institute assess whether the gross and net measures are adequately capturing discrimination in the market. While the discussion addressed this issue, of major concern was the measurement of discrimination in the context of the population of interest and a clear definition of

TABLE 5-2 Proportion of Auditors Receiving Favorable Treatment

White	Minority	
	Favorable	Unfavorable
Favorable	P_{11}	P_{10}[a]
Unfavorable	P_{01}	P_{00}

[a] Gross measure; The net measure is = $P_{10} - P_{01}$.

discrimination. Each of these issues is presented in separate sections of this report.

Some participants expressed their preference for the net measure since it captures the difference in unfavorable treatment of minority and white testers. The gross measure will reveal the number of instances of discrimination against minorities and may appear high; however, the frequency of these instances may be equivalent to that for whites. The net measure will capture this by calibrating the magnitude of the discrimination.

Charles Manski, Board of Trustees Professor, Department of Economics, Northwestern University, and Susan Murphy, Associate Professor, Statistics Department, and Senior Associate Research Scientist, Survey Research Center, University of Michigan, also commented on the breadth of methodological issues in the 2000 HDS and the implications of these issues for measuring discrimination in the national housing market. Their comments included a discussion of the strengths and weaknesses of the current methodology and some alternative methodologies that could be applied.

Manski's discussion addressed measuring the severity or magnitude of discrimination rather than just the occurrence of discrimination. For example, the extent to which the characteristics of minority households must be altered so they appear more qualified than white households could serve as a measure of the magnitude of discrimination. During his comments, Manski also proposed that by collecting richer data, researchers could distinguish between statistical and prejudicial discrimination.

FACTORS AFFECTING HOUSING DISCRIMINATION

The HDS focuses predominantly on economic and family-size characteristics. These attributes of the individual are expected to drive housing needs and thus the units shown or suggested to the auditor. The initial model posits that disparate treatment is due to the individual's race and observable circumstances that could arise during the tester's visit. During the workshop, Urban Institute researchers acknowledged an inability to match auditors on the myriad of possible unobservable characteristics. They stated that their goal was different: to structure a study that could test whether those unobservable characteristics really matter in racially differential treatment of the auditors.

Some participants raised questions about the power of the statistical tests being performed and the need to control for covariates even if the paired-testing methodology appears to control for them. One argument for the use of covariates is that favorable or unfavorable treatment by housing agents may depend on the sector of the housing market or type of transaction observed. The audit methodology results in identical agents observing auditors with similar characteristics. Including the covariates in the model would allow the researchers to observe how the estimated marginal probabilities in Table 5-2 respond to this methodology. Another question raised during the workshop was whether the discussion of power for the statistical tests and the need to control for covariates is necessary in the absence of a clearly defined population. An appropriate model may be one that accounts for the measurement of outcomes that represent a mix of different measured phenomena.

CHARACTERISTICS OF TESTER PAIRS

Several participants expressed concern about the "actual" characteristics of auditors—those not assigned by the test coordinator—and their potential effect on the validity of the test. More specifically, participants asked how test coordinators ensure that the audit pair are believable potential renters or purchasers of the advertised housing unit. The discussion encompassed whether auditors appear able to afford a particular housing unit, as well as how close an auditor's actual residence is to the test site.

An additional concern of workshop participants was heterogeneity among white testers, given that two such testers of differing ancestry may receive very different treatment by a housing agent. Participants suggested that the test coordinator be mindful of this heterogeneity when pairing white with minority testers. Otherwise, the result of the test may reflect not solely minority-white differences, but also the housing agent's perceptions, based on ethnicity or other factors, of a white applicant's attractiveness as a buyer or renter.

In contrast with previous audits, testing agencies participating in HDS 2000 collect actual tester characteristics, such as income, level of education, employment experience, and testing experience. Tester training and test protocols are designed to limit the effect of variation among tester pairs. Participants stressed the importance of addressing the issue of heterogeneity among the auditors, the housing units, and the housing agents. Heterogeneity in any of these elements may have an impact on both the gross and net measures of adverse treatment.

Sanders Korenman, Center for the Study of Business and Government,

Baruch College, City University of New York, commented that auditors' assigned characteristics should reflect the legal definition of discrimination. Researchers should control for attributes that provide legally allowable reasons to deny housing. Researchers may want the minority or white auditor to represent the subset of the minority or white population possessing those allowable characteristics. Korenman believes it would then be unnecessary to control for other differences correlated with race (e.g., language) if these differences are irrelevant to the housing transaction.

Joseph Altonji, Department of Economics, Northwestern University, presented the following model for dealing with the above issues:

$$y_{it} = f(x_{it}, \varepsilon_{it}, z_{it}, v_{it}; R_i)$$

where $_i$ denotes the auditor, and $_t$ denotes the test. In this model, y_{it} is the outcome measure representing favorable or unfavorable treatment (e.g., whether the auditor was shown the unit). The variable x_{it} is a vector containing the characteristics of the auditor that are observed by or known to the researchers and are used to match audit pairs. It includes both assigned and nonassigned attributes, the latter having been collected by the researcher during the application process. The variable ε_{it} is a vector of characteristics of the auditor that are relevant to the agent's assessment of the suitability of the auditor for the unit and are observed by the agent but not used to match audit pairs. The elements of ε_{it} vary across auditors and over time for a given auditor. Both x_{it} and ε_{it} are limited to factors that are legitimate indicators of the suitability of the auditor for the housing unit and may legally be used by the auditor to make judgments. The variables z_{it} and v_{it} represent observed or known and unobserved or unknown characteristics of the unit that determine how the agent weighs the characteristics x_{it} and ε_{it} of the auditor. Finally, the variable R_i denotes the race of the auditor.

In terms of the model, a natural benchmark for discrimination is the situation in which race, R_i plays a role in the agent's decision function given the characteristics of the unit z and v and the characteristics of the auditor x and ε. R will play a role in the auditor's decisions if there is (1) institutional discrimination or racial preference, whether conscious or subconscious, on the part of the agent; and/or (2) the agent uses the race of the auditor to draw inferences about the suitability of the auditor for the unit, such as ability to pay the rent, maintain the unit, or get along with neighbors, or the degree of interest in the unit.

Note that the housing provider may draw inferences about the auditor's suitability for the unit on the basis of the characteristics x and ε. However, if the housing provider uses race to draw any inferences about characteristics that are relevant to the housing transaction, he or she is discriminating.

The audit methodology is to send auditors with the same value of x_{it} to inquire about a housing unit. The fraction of times the outcome is favorable for whites but not for non-whites is sometimes interpreted as a measure of discrimination against non-whites. The fraction of times the outcome is favorable for non-whites but not for whites is sometimes interpreted as a measure of discrimination against whites. The sum of these two fractions is referred to as the gross discrimination rate. The difference between these two fractions is a measure of net discrimination against non-whites.

The problem with the gross measure of discrimination is that random variation across testers in ε_{it}, differences in the distribution of ε_{it} that are related to race, and random variation in z and v between testor visits to a particular unit will lead to differences in the outcomes even though the audit pairs have been matched on x_{it}. (Variation in z and v may arise, for example, from situational changes in the housing provider that occur between the two audit visits, or different weights placed by a particular agent on the characteristics x and ε in the event the auditors see different agents.) That is, the gross measure of discrimination will be positive even if there is no discrimination, and R plays no role in the decision of any of the agents. Note that the variation in z_{it} or in elements of ε_{it} that is observed by the researchers could be accounted for in analyzing the results of the audits. The problem with the net measure of discrimination against non-whites is that it will overstate discrimination to the extent that the values of the uncontrolled auditor characteristics ε_{it} are systematically related to race.

The design and analysis of the audit studies should account for the differences among the auditors and housing providers that are reflected in ε_{it}, z_{it}, and v_{it} in the above model. Altonji offered four comments on how the Urban Institute could address heterogeneity in the study. First, researchers could look for differences in the outcomes of auditors of the same race who have visited similar housing units. This method would assess treatment outcomes within racial groups. Second, researchers could have individual auditors perform multiple tests involving similar units. This method would provide information about the influence of variation across auditors in ε_{it} on the distribution of outcomes. Third, auditors could perform sandwich tests, in which auditors are sent on a test in triples, rather than pairs. The fourth comment is that more information should be gathered about the auditors even if it is not used to form matched pairs. Additional steps should also be taken to gather preferences and characteristics relevant to housing providers. While the 2000 HDS has started to collect these data, more information could be gathered. From this information, the audit researchers could assess which characteristics are most important in matching auditors and assigning attributes. Researchers have considered using the information on the treatment of whites in all the audits to improve estimates of the treatment of whites. These estimates would increase the precision of the net adverse treatment measure.

Murphy's discussion of the methodological aspects of the 2000 HDS also addressed the interaction of auditor characteristics and the structure of audit pairs. She commented that, given the number of audit pairs and the number of visits per audit pair, researchers would not accumulate information within an audit pair because individual characteristics, which may not vary by race, persist across audit pairs. The resulting estimate of discrimination obtained for these audit pairs may be due to individual characteristics that are equally distributed across race or due to discrimination. Provided that researchers have matched testers on characteristics that matter to the housing providers, researchers can obtain better estimates of discrimination by looking across tester pairs.

APPLICATION OF SAMPLING WEIGHTS TO A MEASURE OF HOUSING DISCRIMINATION

A secondary objective of the workshop was for participants to discuss the notion of preserving probability in the selection of advertisements by sampling with probabilities proportional to the size of the audit site. The Urban Institute uses classical population sampling to draw inferences about a population. It is not clear that application of these methods is necessary, however, since the study will not draw the usual theoretical inferences about population parameters. Rather than estimating a known population parameter, the researchers are trying to estimate an underlying phenomenon that exists within the population. The underlying universe encompasses this conceptual model of discrimination and the character or prevalence of discrimination activities that occur in the interaction between two hypothetical individuals.

There was considerable discussion during the workshop about the relevance of sampling weights to the analysis. For certain statistical analyses, weighting is important; however, many participants do not believe sample survey weights are relevant for the type of analysis the Urban Institute is performing. The researchers argued for maintaining weights because advertisements are stratified by weeks. During high-volume weeks, fewer tests are performed. If discriminatory agents represent a large proportion of advertisements during high-volume weeks, they will also be overrepresented in the sample. Not allowing for weighting of the advertisements will ignore the potential bias in the estimate.

Altonji offered another suggestion for addressing weights. He suggested the Urban Institute weight the results using not the advertisements, but the characteristics of the housing unit. The audit results could then be compared with a national database containing the distribution and characteristics of the housing stock in the United States, namely occupancy or vacancy rates. The audit results could be weighted to reflect the expected availability of different housing stock in the market at a particular point in time. It was noted that if weighting is appropriate, approximate weights for the correct population are preferred over equal probability weights that are generated for the incorrect population.

Workshop participants discussed the use of multiple newspapers in the original sampling frame instead of just in the pilot phase. Researchers from the Urban Institute expressed doubt about whether they had placed too much emphasis on the potential overlap in advertising and the fact that a single unit may be advertised in multiple newspapers. Analysts noted that the use of multiple newspapers could not be applied because the Phase I analysis of the 2000 HDS must remain comparable to the 1989 analysis. In discussing potential changes in the design of Phase II, workshop participants suggested the analysts merge all newspaper advertisement sources. Fienberg noted that once the sample has been obtained, analysts can perform the calculation two ways: (1) reweighting according to the sampling probabilities and (2) not reweighting or disregarding the potential overlap. Participants also discussed the feasibility of providing separate estimates for subsets of newspaper sources or for a clearly defined population of newspapers—for example, having the ability to estimate the likelihood of discrimination for the major newspapers in a particular area without concern for drawing inferences about the U.S. housing market. Several variations could be explored, including oversampling of underrepresented housing unit types.

A recurring theme throughout the workshop was characterization of the housing market. Specification of the population of housing units has implications for the inferences drawn, as well as the appropriate weighting scheme. Workshop participants proposed that while the U.S. housing market is a candidate for the population, it may not reflect the true population of interest to the researchers. More specifically, if researchers are interested in discrimination against minority households, the population might be restricted to housing units in which this subgroup would be interested. The entire U.S. housing market may be the housing choice set of minority groups, or that set may be restricted to particular housing types. One proposal for restricting the housing market was to segment it by housing costs or affordability.

METHODOLOGICAL IMPLICATIONS
OF THE PHASE II DESIGN

Tom Louis of the RAND Corporation addressed methodological implications of the Phase II design. He discussed the importance of identifying a set of primary goals for the study in a nonstatistical way. For instance, if the design includes the whole population, however defined, what summaries will be obtained, and what will they mean? Without being concerned with sample weights or statistical tests, what do the estimates mean, and do they provide the information needed? Once the proper estimates have been obtained and their meaning understood, the problem can be designed with the appropriate weights and statistical model. A premise of the audit design is that the survey design and weights can be extrapolated to a population. Inherent in the variables of interest is that these extrapolations capture contrasts in the population. The design should serve the objective of comparing treatment between white and minority home seekers. The weights will provide metropolitan-area estimates based on the distribution of advertisements within the sample relative to the population.

Louis also discussed the importance of weights applied to the sample of advertisements. If the contrast in white and minority treatment measured by some metric (e.g., the difference or odds ratio) has either no or low interaction with attributes used to form strata or sampling frames, the within-sample weights are adjusted. Louis addressed the design of later study phases in view of the findings from earlier phases. He suggested Phase II could serve the objective of providing reasonable estimates of the variance components associated with auditors, housing providers, and advertisement sources. The later phases of the study would rely on exploration of the interactions between audit pairs and other methodological concerns identified in earlier phases.

Louis suggested that a more appropriate primary goal of the HDS might be to better understand transactions in the general housing market rather than to conduct a definitive study representing the population of housing market transactions. These statistical and policy-related decisions on the study design and objectives will determine how samples are allocated. Louis's remarks also addressed matching of audit pairs and its implications for the interpretation of audit results. He expressed concern about the large variance component for the matched pairs on the one hand and the inability to properly model tester heterogeneity on the other. He suggested that matching auditors on the wrong attributes—characteristics that have high variance components—could be worse than not attempting to match auditors at all. He did not suggest abandoning the matching of auditor pairs. Rather, he stressed matching on important attributes and formulating a model that would allow for the specification of covariance adjustments.

As noted earlier, sandwich tests, in which two auditors of the same race view the advertised unit—one prior to and the other after the minority tester—can provide important information about differential treatment in housing transactions. Louis noted that similar information could be obtained without performing an actual sandwich test. By combining information within racial groups across audits for similar housing units, researchers could explore variation within racial groups, particularly for matched characteristics. Analyses across audit sites could also provide information needed in low-population sites, such as underserved communities. For some sites, the definition of an underserved community restricts the study to small sample sizes. Louis proposed that a mix of design- and model-based analyses that incorporates results from various test sites could help in obtaining estimates within smaller sites. Participants did not offer definitive ways of addressing these issues, but noted the importance of raising them.

Korenman presented several methodological implications of the Phase II design. He emphasized the need to assess the quality of an estimator with respect to how the researchers and other members of the housing community will use the measure. He also mentioned the importance of having a definition of discrimination and identifying what the study attempts to measure. He reiterated two uses of the latter: providing a benchmark for racial discrimination in U.S. housing markets and identifying target communities for enforcement audits.

Returning to an issue discussed earlier, Korenman also addressed which measure—gross or net adverse treatment—is most appropriate for estimating discrimination. He noted that while the objective is not to provide one measure, but rather various components of an overall benchmark, each component should be a credible and reliable estimate. He noted the importance of having the gross and net measures capture the desired phenomenon and move in directions consistent with what is known about housing discrimination from other sources. One aspect of this issue is the need to measure adverse treatment relative to the legal definition of discrimination or adverse treatment. Korenman stated that, consistent with the legal definition, researchers could assign profiles and match testers on attributes that constitute legal bases for differential treatment.

Korenman also expressed the need for a better understanding of the processes that generate variation across time and space in the measurement of housing discrimination. He did not propose that such analysis be added to the scope of the HDS, but observed that the issues involved are important and call for some caution in interpreting results.

Korenman commented as well on the proposed remedies for selection bias in the newspaper sampling methodology. In addition to underrepresented areas, the sampling frame may underrepresent housing unit types (e.g., rent control units). The modified sampling frame would still miss some unit types. Participants discussed capturing available housing stock by linking vacancy rates with actual rentals or turnovers to buttress the newspaper selection methodology. Korenman commented on the screening call, in which a white tester calls about the housing unit to determine whether it is still available. He asked what information is retained from such calls and whether researchers could test to see whether the race of the auditor making the initial screening call matters.

Finally, participants discussed the implications of changes in demographics for the legal definition of discrimination and the audit methodology. Some participants commented on the basis of casual observations that discrimination against whites may be more prevalent in some high-minority housing markets. Also, in some housing markets where whites are a small minority of the population, white-minority testing may not make sense; rather, it may be more appropriate to pair a second- or third-generation Hispanic or Asian auditor with an African American auditor. These multiracial and multiethnic pairs may be more reflective of the actual housing search pattern in these types of communities. The 2000 census represents the first time respondents could multiply identify on race and ethnicity on a full national scale. Data obtained from the census may indicate potential modifications to the paired-testing methodology. Participants raised the issues of (1) how to measure discrimination in housing markets with changing demographics, and (2) whether sending individual auditors as opposed to pairs of auditors representing a household would better capture the housing market.

6

Auditing Discrimination in Underserved Communities

As noted earlier, underserved communities are those portions of the housing market that are not included in the HDS sampling frame used to select test sites or newspaper advertisements. For purposes of the 2000 HDS, there are two types of underserved communities: (1) neighborhoods that are underrepresented among advertisements in large metropolitan area newspapers, and (2) smaller metropolitan areas with 25,000 to 100,000 residents. In discussing the question of how discrimination in these communities can be audited, participants addressed issues of racial residential concentration, racial steering, racial preferences for neighborhood racial composition, and the distinction between statistical discrimination and individual incidences of discrimination.

Reflecting on her own research, Nancy Denton noted an apparent middle-class bias to using a sample of advertisements to construct the audit. This potential bias raises issues that are both statistical and substantive. Denton linked the auditors who are recruited to perform tests to actual home seekers in underserved communities. She observed that if the definition of underserved includes only communities that are missed by the methodology used to select advertisements, researchers have failed to recognize that these areas include poor communities that are underserved in other ways as well. They are underserved by realtors, who do not want to advertise them, and by banks, which do not want to provide potential home buyers with mortgages. These communities are also underserved by entities that are indirectly related to housing opportunities but potentially related to housing choices and search patterns, such as businesses and municipal services. Transportation access and education resources are also limited in these communities.

The varying extent to which these communities are underserved has methodological implications. In some poor communities, no housing is advertised; these communities will be missed regardless of the sampling methodology. Similarly, housing opportunities in gated communities and some working-class communities are unadvertised. Denton also noted that some housing is advertised in non-English language newspapers because the advertiser is targeting immigrants or non-American applicants, and some housing is not advertised because the landlord does not want applicants of a different race. As noted earlier, these housing units may not be captured by the expanded methodology proposed for Phase II of the study. Additionally, Denton suggested that researchers should consider whether the auditors could realistically assume the identities of potential home seekers in underserved communities, whose members may possess characteristics that are difficult for an auditor from a major metropolitan area to assume or portray. Moreover, housing search patterns may differ across income levels, and these differences can have implications for matching auditors and assigning auditor profiles. Denton commented that housing transactions for marginally qualified and overly qualified applicants are also very different, and these differences have implications for the audit results, particularly in terms of unmeasured heterogeneity. The question arises of whether auditors are paired well enough to diminish the effect of this heterogeneity and the potential discrepancies between auditors' actual characteristics and their assigned profiles. Participants recognized that auditors are extensively trained to portray various types of home seekers and that their assigned profiles may require them to depict individuals with attributes dissimilar to their own. Denton suggested, however, that it is important to consider whether auditors are trained well enough or inherently capable of assuming identities that are beyond their scope of knowledge. She noted that these issues are particularly salient when auditors visit certain kinds of communities, such as low-income or mono-ethnic communities.

Denton cautioned researchers to consider potential problems with sending auditors from fair housing agencies in larger metropolitan areas to smaller underserved areas, which are unlikely to have a fair housing agency. Additionally, she posed several questions with regard to those agencies' recruitment and training methods: Can a middle-income auditor with no children effectively portray a low-income single mother? Can an employed auditor who has never received public assistance effectively portray a home seeker who has just obtained his or her first job after receiving public assistance for many years? Can a low- or moderate-income auditor effectively audit housing units that require very high incomes? Denton expressed her belief that there are limits to the auditors' portrayals, and that auditor training does not eliminate these limitations.

An additional drawback of the current methodology for auditing underserved communities relates to potential differences in housing search methods as compared with major metropolitan areas. Prior research by Denton and others has shown that residents in underserved communities are less likely to use a real estate agent during their housing search. They may also be less likely to drive around several communities to locate a desired neighborhood or housing unit. According to Denton, audit protocols and auditor profiles must take these potential differences into account.

In her concluding remarks, Denton suggested that researchers should consider substantive issues such as those outlined above before addressing the technical aspects of auditing and measuring discrimination. She stressed that, while it is important to develop a valid, scientifically defensible estimate of the extent of housing discrimination in the national market, researchers will be unable to derive a proper estimate if they limit the scope of audit studies to the middle of the housing market.

EFFECT OF NEIGHBORHOOD RACIAL PREFERENCE ON INTERPRETATION OF AUDIT RESULTS

Lawrence Bobo, Department of Sociology, Harvard University, discussed his research in Los Angeles on urban inequality and the work of others in this research area. Bobo's research assessed residents' preferences for the racial composition of their neighborhoods. Results of the study indicate that preferences for the racial composition of neighborhoods are related to race. Bobo noted that the study did not lead to recommendations on how to sample housing units or assign auditors, but that its results have implications for the interpretation of results of the HDS, particularly with regard to rates of housing discrimination.

Bobo's data indicate clearly that in the general housing market, some communities are more likely to accept or reject particular racial groups. These attitudes are held by both majority and minority residents and can have implications for the way applicants of a given race are treated in a housing market transaction. Research on racial residential segregation also confirms that many neighborhoods are racially typified (e.g., as a Hispanic neighborhood). Such typifying affects whether certain groups will pursue housing in these neighborhoods. Bobo expressed concern that the current method of sampling advertisements does not account for these kinds of community dynamics and the interaction between racial preference and housing search patterns. He suggested that it is insufficient to randomly sample advertisements in local community-based newspapers because different racial groups may consider varying segments of the housing market. Some racial groups may exclude housing opportunities in certain neighborhoods from their housing search. Research on racial residential segregation might help identify neighborhoods or communities that are not included in the housing search of certain racial groups.

A participant asked about the implications of the Los Angeles study for the "tipping point" of a community—the point at which people start moving out because of increases in the proportion of minority residents—and the relationship to housing availability. Neighborhood racial preference could affect the vacancy rates in particular neighborhoods. Specifically, the sample of advertisements may include a higher proportion of mixed or racially transitional neighborhoods as majority households move out because of increases in the proportion of minorities. The sampling methodology may miss stable all-white or all-minority neighborhoods where there is less movement.

In response to Bobo's comments, Margery Turner of the Urban Institute stated that empirical experience from the 1989 HDS suggests that minority communities, especially those in the central city, are underrepresented in the HDS newspaper advertisement sample. It is not known whether protected white communities in the suburbs are also underrepresented. It is clear, however, that middle- and high-income minority communities were underrepresented in the 1989 sample of advertisements. Participants discussed the need for data on the turnover rate for rental and sales housing for both racially stable and transitional communities. While researchers can obtain information on housing stock, basic turnover rate data do not exist on a national level.

A participant asked whether the 1989 HDS provided some evidence that housing agents advertise units they are willing to show to anyone, regardless of race. This behavior would result in a lower incidence of racial steering. Turner responded that because minority and mixed neighborhoods were underrepresented in the 1989 newspaper advertisement sample, minority auditors were generally shown housing units in white neighborhoods. Researchers noted that in 1989 there was some steering to lower-value neighborhoods, but not much steering to neighborhoods with a higher proportion of minorities, because the latter were underrepresented in the sample.

RACIAL STEERING

Bobo noted that the existence of racial steering has implications for the current HDS study design and interpretation. If real estate agents have, and act upon, assumptions about housing seekers' racial preferences in residence, individual home seekers will not be shown housing units in certain neighborhoods as a result.

A participant presented an alternative motivation for racial steering by housing providers, suggesting they may be motivated by profit maximization rather than racial prejudice or agents' perceptions of client or community preferences. Housing providers may be more likely to steer white customers to white neighborhoods because they think doing so will minimize the amount of time it takes to fill vacant units. Housing agents operating in this manner will be less worried about the preferences of minority applicants. They will, however, be concerned with the effect of renting or selling to an African American customer on their current or potential clients in white neighborhoods. Evidence of this behavior may be found in steering of white households away from minority neighborhoods or steering of minority households away from white neighborhoods. Bobo noted it is not clear that this form of racial steering hurts whites, unless one takes a broader view of discrimination and its general effect on society.

According to Bobo, the above processes are confirmed by respondents' views on neighborhood desirability as reported in the Los Angeles area study. Many white residents considered affluent majority African American communities to be less desirable than lower-valued white communities. Community-held views of neighborhood racial composition may therefore propagate racial residential segregation. These results suggest that the random selection of advertisements from newspapers does not account for neighborhood self-selection exhibited by actual home seekers.

Bobo commented further that the steering of white households may actually hurt African American homeowners by changing the demand for their housing. Urban Institute researchers cited evidence from the 1989 HDS that a requested housing unit's characteristics and location served as a signal to real estate agents and housing providers with regard to the type of neighborhood to which the requester should be directed. The researchers believe it is important to consider the broad methodology used for picking an advertised unit and selecting two auditors who are requesting that unit. Requesting an advertised unit appears to influence behavior in a specific way: if an auditor asks for a unit in a certain type of neighborhood, he or she will be more likely to view additional units in that type of neighborhood. Real estate agents are prompted by any information they can obtain to serve their customer, but they do not apply that information in a race-neutral manner. Bobo noted that observed steering behaviors based on requests for advertised units vary by race.

ISSUES SPECIFIC TO ASIAN AMERICAN AND AMERICAN INDIAN POPULATIONS

As noted in Chapter 1, an important, new goal of the 2000 HDS is to develop estimates of housing discrimination for Asian Americans and American Indians. Workshop participants addressed the potential impact of testing involving these populations.

Min Zhou, Office of Educational Research and Improvement, U.S. Department of Education, offered some comments about the study design and substantive issues related to auditing within the Asian American and American Indian communities. She noted that the potential bias against immigrants has implications for audits performed in metropolitan areas. Moreover, metropolitan areas with high proportions of immigrant residents often have a different housing market structure from that of other metropolitan areas. For example, minority immigrants tend to concentrate in certain neighborhoods and to have their own housing market. As a result, there may be several housing submarkets operating within a metropolitan area: (1) exclusively majority, (2) exclusively African American or Hispanic, (3) mixed or "open," and (4) exclusively Asian American. In addition, Asian ethnic groups further segment the latter housing market. The dynamics of these housing markets are different from those of the general housing market.

Zhou explained that real estate agencies are a very important part of the Chinese and Korean ethnic economy and that they tend to target particular ethnic groups in advertising. Advertising patterns within the Asian American submarkets suggest there may also be discrimination against other ethnic and racial groups. Asian Americans locate available housing by speaking with other members of their ethnic group or reading ethnic newspapers. Since these newspapers are written in Chinese or Korean, responding to their advertisements may not represent a realistic point of entry into the market for auditors from other ethnic groups. Zhou stressed that researchers must recognize these alternative points of entry because they are where a substantial proportion of inquiries by Asian American home seekers begin. The current HDS newspaper sampling methodology would miss these sources, but including them in the expanded sampling frame might not be appropriate. Thus, according to Zhou, there are portions of the housing market that are inaccessible by the audit study design.

Zhou suggested expanding the concept of discrimination. The current study estimates mainly discrimination by whites against African Americans, Hispanics, Asian Americans, and American Indians. It does not explore the pattern of discrimination exhibited by Asian or Hispanic housing providers. Zhou's definition of discrimination is more varied because it includes Asians discriminating against Asians, Hispanics, and African Americans.

In terms of white discrimination against Asian Americans, Zhou observed that Asian Americans who speak with an accent can be viewed as foreign and treated on the basis of stereotypes associated with foreigners. She used as an example the stereotype that immigrant Asians have the financial resources to purchase housing with cash or make a substantial down payment. In addition, there are negative stereotypes associated with working-class Asians and perceived differences in lifestyle. Thus, the stereotypes applied may be positive or negative and may result in differential behavior by the housing agent.

Zhou observed that many Asian Americans are unfamiliar with fair housing laws and are not aware of their rights under the Fair Housing Act. She noted there is substantial anecdotal evidence of racial steering for Asian American households. This steering is carried out by housing providers, as well as friends and family of the home seeker, and is perceived as being helpful. Zhou also cited the increasing tendency of real estate agencies to hire Asian or Hispanic agents. It is unclear, however, whether the objective is to systematically steer or to legitimately assist home seekers.

The amount of money applicants are asked to provide for a down payment or security deposit is another example of housing market discrimination against Asian Americans. While overall mortgage denial rates may be lower for Asian Americans than for other minority groups, Asian Americans may pay a higher proportional down payment. This larger percentage will increase the chances that the mortgage will be originated, but may not be viewed as discrimination when analyzing market-level data.

A participant asked whether the extent of heterogeneity among Asian Americans prevents researchers from measuring discrimination in that group. Zhou responded that the HDS does not include sufficient observations to explore discrimination across ethnic groups within the Asian community, and that case studies would be more effective for this purpose. She noted further that there is considerable diversity within the Hispanic population, but that Hispanics and African Americans may have common historical or cultural experiences that result in similarities in their discrimination experiences. Thus differences in language, religion, and national origin among Asian populations present substantial difficulties for interpreting audit results.

Responding to Zhou, Stephen Fienberg noted that her observations imply there are separate universes with distinct sampling frames from which measurements are made. Housing availability notices and housing market transactions may be structured differently in these markets and vary across test sites. To the extent that these structures are not known and sampling of advertisements is not viable, many underserved communities will be missed. Joseph Altonji suggested a way of addressing multiple listing sources for advertisements and differential access to advertisements in some sources: (1) combine advertisements from all newspaper sources—including non-English language papers, and (2) use audit results to assess which advertisement sources are open to all groups regardless of race. Assuming advertisements in papers of a certain language are open only to that ethnic group (e.g., Korean or Chinese), researchers could draw conclusions about equal access for underserved populations. Altonji added that the assumption might not be appropriate for Spanish-language papers that serve Hispanic communities because a larger proportion of the non-Hispanic population speaks Spanish than speaks Chinese or Korean. Conclusions about the penetration of various sources into underserved communities and the reasonableness of sending majority auditors to units advertised in ethnic papers may require going beyond the auditing framework to assess discrimination against particular ethnic groups.

The discussion of auditing in Asian communities also addressed the question of whether the paradigm of paired testing makes sense in segregated housing markets that attempt to accept only Asian ethnic groups. Some participants suggested that the best way to understand this issue is within the framework of varying degrees of discrimination. In this conceptualization, there is some discrimination that is essentially benign and serves to meet the needs of populations underserved by the general housing market. This discrimination is viewed as beneficial because it is a parochial phenomenon, initiated by people who are trying to help individuals who might otherwise be discriminated against by the majority group. On the other hand, some participants stressed that every act of discrimination, regardless of the initiating or benefiting group, is legally wrong.

Research confirms that housing choice and household neighborhood preferences are issues within Asian communities. Focus group research associated with the Los Angeles study addressed issues of housing, employment, and intergroup relations. Within the Korean focus groups, each individual found his or her job through one source—the *Korean Daily News.* This finding was not characteristic of any other group, including the Chinese focus group, whose members, like those of the Korean group, were 100 percent foreign born. The focus group results for the Los Angeles study also inform the design of the HDS audits. For populations with a large proportion of foreign-born members, the major metropolitan newspaper will not fully capture the housing dynamics faced by underserved individuals.

There was a brief discussion of auditing in American Indian and rural communities. Participants considered the idea of addressing acknowledged difficulties in auditing in rural communities by linking auxiliary studies in Phase II with other data collected by the Urban Institute. The question of how American Indian communities are defined was raised. Researchers responded that the communities to be audited are not on tribal land, but in a fairly large metropolitan area and one small metropolitan area that adjoins tribal lands. To achieve adequate coverage of available housing in these areas, the newspaper sampling frame combines up to ten rural and small-town newspapers. The audits will assess whether the basic measures of differential treatment apply in American Indian communities.

The Urban Institute researchers commented on pilot studies in American Indian communities. Pilot testing has revealed that for American Indians, the definition of available housing stock must be expanded beyond the existing protocol to include manufactured housing. American Indian populations tend to be concentrated in small, rural metropolitan areas in which this form of housing is more prevalent. Further, this housing type is not typically advertised in major metropolitan newspapers. Researchers plan to consult with the local fair housing agency to find a point of entry into these underserved communities. Additional sources for available housing stock are community newspapers and postings in community centers or on the Internet.

Results from the pilot studies will provide substantial information about how to sample beyond a single metropolitan newspaper in small communities and adjoining rural counties. Researchers also expect to learn a great deal about whether and how to recruit American Indians as auditors. The pilot studies will be informative as well about the feasibility of sending white auditors into adjoining counties that have a high proportion of American Indian households. Results from the smaller pilot studies will be used to determine the feasibility of replicating the study of these communities on a larger scale.

Participants asked whether the underserved communities would be analyzed separately given the number of audits performed. The audit report will include simple comparisons and will address differences in patterns of discrimination and the existence of a racial dimension to those differences. Participants also inquired about the extent to which HUD is interested in alternative methodology that could make it possible to estimate discrimination in underserved communities and provide supplementary information for the HDS on the relationship between race and housing search patterns, as well as other housing market characteristics. In addition, participants discussed the importance of research studies addressing the identification of an unbiased point of entry into the market that would allow for comparisons, measurement, and analysis of issues related to the sampling design and model estimates and other aspects of the study design. Housing research studies focused on these issues could lead to improvements in the HDS audit design.

References

Fix, M., G. Galster, and R. Struyk
  1993 An overview of auditing for discrimination. In *Clear and Convincing Evidence: Testing for Discrimination in America.* M. Fix and R. Struyk, eds. Washington, D.C.: Urban Institute Press.

Heckman, J.
  1998 Detecting discrimination. *Journal of Economic Perspectives* (12):101-116.

Massey, D.S., and G. Lundy
  1998 Use of Black English and Racial Discrimination in Urban Housing Markets: New Methods and Findings. Unpublished Paper, Population Studies Center, University of Pennsylvania.

Ondrich, J., S. Ross, and J. Yinger
  2000 How common is housing discrimination? Improving on traditional measures. *Journal of Urban Economics* (47):470-500.

Ross, S.
  2000 Paired Testing and the 2000 Housing Discrimination Study. Paper prepared for the Workshop on the Measurement of Discrimination in Housing, National Research Council, Washington, D.C., September 22-23, 2000.

Appendix A

Paired Testing and the 2000 Housing Discrimination Survey

Stephen L. Ross

This paper was prepared for a National Research Council workshop on the use of paired testing to study racial and ethnic discrimination in housing markets. A primary motivation for the conduct of this workshop was to examine methodological issues surrounding the use of newspaper advertisements for initiating tests. This methodology was used in the 1989 Housing Discrimination Study (HDS) and is being used in Phase I of the 2000 HDS. The approach involves a two-stage sampling of newspaper advertisements from medium-sized and large U.S. metropolitan areas with substantial minority populations. In the first stage, metropolitan areas are selected as test sites, and tests are conducted within a site on the basis of a sampling of advertisements from the major metropolitan newspaper.

This paper is organized into two major sections. The first introduces the concept of paired testing and reviews the major issues surrounding its use. The second provides a brief summary of the design of Phase I of the 2000 HDS, including a more detailed discussion of the advertisement-based sampling approach and potential alternatives.

Stephen L. Ross is an associate professor of economics in the Department of Economics, University of Connecticut.

PAIRED TESTING METHODOLOGY

Basic Approach

The basic logic behind a paired test for discrimination is fairly straightforward. Two testers, one white and one minority, are matched on characteristics that are relevant to the market transaction being considered. Each tester is then sent to inquire about a market transaction under fairly controlled and highly similar circumstances. For example, in the case of rental housing, the two testers would be similar in age and physical appearance, assigned the same income and family status, and sent to inquire about the same rental unit and/or to the same rental agency using a common protocol. The result of each tester's inquiry and the treatment experienced are reported and documented in isolation from the other tester. The two testers' experiences are combined and compared at a later date by an independent third party.

Any differences between the paired testers' experiences is considered evidence of adverse or differential treatment. Paired testing is designed to measure the level or frequency of adverse treatment discrimination in a given market, where adverse treatment discrimination is defined as instances in which the treatment of an individual is adversely affected by his or her race, ethnicity, or other legally protected characteristic. Paired testing measures the level or frequency observed based on a specific protocol for sampling the market. Therefore, the testing cannot measure the actual impact of discrimination on individuals in the marketplace. For example, if real estate agents steer minority home buyers away from discriminatory lenders, a paired test of the mortgage market will not capture the mitigating effect of this behavior.

In addition, paired testing will not uncover the existence of adverse impact discrimination in a given market. Adverse impact discrimination is defined as follows. A firm or a set of firms in a market engages in many economic transactions, and for each transaction there is a relevant population of reasonable candidates. Adverse impact discrimination occurs when the policy of one or a number of firms places the minority group within the relevant population at a disadvantage relative to the majority even when the policy is applied uniformly, and this policy cannot be justified by business necessity. Naturally, this type of discrimination cannot be detected by testing because the policy is applied uniformly, and systematic racial differences in treatment may not exist.

Paired Testing Versus Analysis of Market Outcomes

As mentioned earlier, the key difference between findings based on testing data and those based on analysis of market outcomes is that testing isolates the incidence or level of discrimination observed when pairs of testers are assigned to enter a market following exogenous sampling and testing protocols. This structure raises issues concerning the relevance of the observed patterns of adverse treatment. The sampling and testing protocols may not yield a sample of market entries that is representative of the types of experiences typically observed in the marketplace. For example, in the 1989 HDS, a sample of units advertised in major metropolitan areas may not have been representative of the available housing stock. Likewise, the testing protocol, which required testers to walk into a real estate agency and refer to an advertisement they had found in the newspaper, may not resemble the approach followed by most consumers when entering the housing market. Second, testers are sampled in a nonrandom manner based on a hiring process, which may lead to systematic differences between the population of white and minority testers. Finally, results based on testing data ignore the mitigating influence of minority attempts to avoid discrimination or mitigate the impact of experienced discriminatory behavior.

While these concerns are important when interpreting the results of a testing study, the design features that lead to these concerns are also important positive attributes of testing as a research tool. Studies of market outcomes often face considerable design challenges because unobserved individual characteristics may influence key determinants of treatment, such as income, education, and work history, and also influence treatment directly (endogeneity bias), and these unobservables may influence individuals' choices concerning whether and how to enter a specific market (selection bias). For example, Ondrich et al. (2001) find that the initial request of a potential home buyer has a large influence on the treatment experienced, but such a request is typically unobserved in market data. Many of the observable determinants of treatment are assigned and therefore uncorrelated with tester unobservables. In addition, the protocols eliminate any possibility of selection bias by exogenously sampling from a population and by establishing a testing protocol that is followed carefully by both testers.

Of course, actual characteristics of testers, such as education or work experience, may influence their behavior during a test and as a result affect their treatment. If so, these characteristics may bias the results of a testing study because of across-race differences in these characteristics or the non-random assignment of testers to particular tests. Naturally, the goal of the testing protocols and tester training is to minimize the variation in behavior across testers, which should in turn limit the influence of actual characteristics on testers' behavior and therefore on observed treatment. A well-designed paired-testing study may in fact dramatically limit the potential for omitted-variable bias by insulating observed outcomes from individual characteristics that are often difficult to observe or record and potentially correlated with race within the population. Heckman and Siegelman (1993) and Ondrich et al. (2000, 2001) test whether testers are heterogeneous over attributes that influence treatment in employment and housing tests, respectively. The evidence for employment tests is mixed, and the evidence for housing tests does not support the conclusion that testers are heterogeneous in a way that influences treatment.

Moreover, the interpretation of observed racial differences is much more straightforward with testing data than with market data. First, tests for discrimination based on market data completely incorporate the effects of any compensating behavior by the individuals being discriminated against even if such behavior imposes additional costs on the minority group. For example, in mortgage markets, a home buyer may avoid potential discrimination in underwriting by seeking out a higher-cost lender with lower standards. Alternatively, a home buyer may obtain a mortgage from a second lender after being discriminated against, but only after losing his or her first-choice home.

Second, observed racial differences in testing data represent adverse treatment against minorities. On the other hand, analyses of market data often combine the outcomes of individuals who engaged in economic transactions with different firms. Even in a model that controls for all relevant individual characteristics, observed racial differences may arise because on average, minorities engage in economic transactions with firms that have different policies, standards, or prices from those of firms that are typically engaged by whites. If these behavioral differences between firms are not justified by business necessity, the observed racial differences would be described as adverse impact discrimination. However, the behavioral differences may arise because the firms operate in different market segments and therefore represent legitimate business practices, in which case the observed racial differences in the market should not be classified as discrimination. Market analyses often cannot distinguish among these three explanations for racial differences in outcomes (see Ross and Yinger, 1999).

The paired structure of the tests also provides two significant advantages. First, the comparison is based on observationally equivalent individuals being treated differently by the same firm or individual, and the results of such comparisons carry considerable narrative power in both legal and policy arenas. Second, the structure of a paired test results in substantial statistical power for detecting discrimination. Specifically, the likelihood of similar treatment of two testers is very high because they have the same relevant characteristics and have been sent into very similar circumstances. The high probability of similar treatment decreases the likelihood that differences in treatment arise by chance and increases the ability to statistically isolate systematic adverse treatment of a given group.

Measuring Adverse Treatment

The results of a test are typically described using two measures of adverse treatment—gross and net. Gross adverse treatment is the portion or fraction of tests in which the white tester received more favorable treatment than the minority tester based on the reports of the two testers and a predetermined criterion for favorable treatment. Net adverse treatment is the fraction of tests in which whites were favored minus the fraction of tests in which minorities were favored. If the treatment can be described by a binary variable in which favorable treatment for one tester is recorded as a one and unfavorable treatment as a zero, the white tester is favored over the minority tester when the former records a one and the latter a zero. If the treatment is described by an ordinal or continuous variable, the white tester is favored if he or she records a higher value than the minority tester. For continuous variables, a threshold will usually be established, and the testers are assumed to have experienced equal treatment if the difference in white and minority treatment does not exceed the threshold.

Both the gross and net measures of adverse treatment may provide misleading estimates of the actual extent of discrimination even within the sampling frame being examined by the set of tests. The gross measure is likely to include differences in treatment that arise simply because the testers' visits differed in some unobserved way, and it may therefore overstate discrimination. The net measure is intended to correct for this problem by subtracting instances in which the white tester experiences adverse treatment relative to the minority tester. The net measure is constructed under the assumption that adverse treatment against the white tester occurs only because the testers' visits differed, and so adverse treatment against the white tester provides an accurate measure of the number of instances of minority adverse treatment that arose because the testers' visits differed. In some cases, however, adverse treatment of the white tester may have been based on the tester's race. For example, in a housing test, the white tester may not be shown a unit in a minority neighborhood because he or she is white. In this case, the net measure will understate discrimination because the frequency of white adverse treatment overstates the frequency of minority adverse treatment that arose from differences between the two testers' visits. For alternative discussions of net and gross adverse treatment, see Fix et al. (1993) and Heckman and Siegelman (1993).

This problem may be avoided by the use of a three-person test, often called a "sandwich test." In a sandwich test, two white and one minority tester are matched, assigned similar characteristics, and sent into the same market conditions. In this test, the potential exists for two individuals of the same race to receive differential treatment. These differences in treatment cannot be caused by race and must have arisen because of differences between the visits. Therefore, these differences can be used to construct a net measure that measures discrimination more accurately. Specifically, the frequency of adverse treatment of one white tester relative to the other, which can arise only because of differences in the two testers' visits, is subtracted from the frequency of adverse treatment of the minority tester relative to a white tester.

Alternatively, additional information concerning each test might be used to uncover the extent of discrimination experienced in a sample of tests. For example, in the housing market, information may be available concerning whether the white and minority testers saw the same agent during their visits or whether the advertised unit was in a neighborhood with a large percentage of minority residents. If the gross measure declines dramatically for the subsample in which the testers saw the same agent, that measure must seriously overstate discrimination. Alternatively, if the vast majority of white-favored tests occur when the advertised units are located in neighborhoods with large minority populations, the net measure must understate discrimination.

Ondrich et al. (2000) use this information and the structure provided by a parametric model to estimate upper and lower bounds on housing discrimination using the 1989 HDS. The frequency measures of adverse treatment discussed above can be thought of as simple nonparametric estimates of the probability of adverse treatment. The same probabilities can be predicted using the estimates from a parametric model of a test. A paired test can be modeled as two separate decisions by an economic agent, where the unobservables associated with those two decisions share a common component because of the paired nature of the test. One possible specification is a bivariate probit in which each equation models the treatment of one tester, and there is a correlation between the treatments received by the pair. Unobservable differences between the two testers' visits are likely to decrease the correlation between the treatments and increase the predicted probability of adverse treatment of the minority tester relative to the white tester—the gross measure. Ondrich et al. (2000) control for differences between the visits by increasing the correlation between the equations to eliminate differences between the visits and revise the gross measure downward.

Implementation Issues

In the abstract, the strategy of sending a pair of testers to attempt the same market transaction following a common protocol appears simple and fairly straightforward. However, many market transactions are quite complex, involving substantially more interactions than simply a negotiation of prices and quantities, and only limited information concerning the nature and form of these transactions may be available. A testing effort will be successful only if the design sends testers into the market in a systematic and realistic manner.

The first design step for a testing effort is to define a point of entry into the market. This point of entry becomes the basis for sampling the market. A test must be initiated by random or stratified sampling from a well-defined population. For example, in the case of a rental housing market, tests might be initiated on the basis of sampling the population of available rental units or the population of agents who represent rental properties. However, there is no reliable source for the population of available units or even the population of agents for rental properties. Even if the population of agents could be observed for a specific metropolitan area, it is unlikely that any information would be available on the volume of business handled by individual agents. An alternative approach used in the 1989 HDS was to sample from the population of housing advertisements appearing in the major metropolitan newspaper, which was easily observable and provided a reasonable mechanism for entering the market.

Once a test has been initiated, the testers must approach the economic agent who has been sampled or who represents the property, job, or good that has been sampled. A tester's approach should be consistent with both the sampling frame discussed above and approaches commonly witnessed by the economic agent being tested. In the case of the 1989 HDS, testers walked into a real estate agency and inquired about a unit in an advertisement that had been selected randomly from the newspaper. This behavior would be expected by real estate agents since advertisements are typically used to attract customers, and this protocol also explicitly tied the treatment experienced to the unit that had been sampled. In some markets, however, a realistic point of entry is more difficult to implement. For example, independent mortgage brokers would be a very difficult group to test because many mortgage brokers obtain the majority of their business through referrals from builders or real estate agents. These brokers would notice if they and their competitors simultaneously experienced a substantial increase in direct contacts either by phone or by walk-in.

Recent Applications

1989 Housing Discrimination Study

The 1989 HDS was a major national study of discrimination against African Americans and Hispanics in both the rental and sales housing markets. The study sampled newspaper advertisements in 25 metropolitan areas to produce national estimates of housing discrimination. For each advertisement sampled, a pair of testers who were matched by age and gender were assigned an appropriate income level for the sampled housing. The testers were then sent to the advertising agency to inquire about the advertised unit and request to see it and any other similar available housing.

The 1989 HDS was designed to measure the national incidence of discrimination arising during visits by qualified home seekers to a sample of units advertised for sale or rent in major metropolitan area newspapers across the United States. The sample of advertised units was drawn in two stages. First, a sample of metropolitan areas was drawn from major U.S. metropolitan areas with a central city population of 100,000 or more and a substantial proportion of African Americans and/or Hispanics based on the 1980 census (12 percent African American and/or 7 percent Hispanic). Additional tests were conducted in five of these sites to support more in-depth analysis. These sites were chosen with certainty based on their substantial minority population to increase the statistical precision of the national estimates. Each selected area became an African American-white and/or a Hispanic-white site for the 1989 HDS. Within each site, weekly samples of advertisements were drawn randomly from the Sunday newspaper.

A system of weights was generated to represent the inverse of the probability of selection for any given advertisement and to adjust for over-sampling and nonresponse. These weights represented the joint probability of site selection and advertisement selection within a site, controlling for advertisement volume from week to week, saturation of the housing market within any week, and attrition within the sample of advertisements. Weighted racial differences in treatment provide an estimate of average adverse treatment in a national sample of advertisements.

The study provided estimates of adverse treatment for a variety of measures covering housing availability, sales effort, terms and conditions (rental only), and financing assistance (sales only). For the treatment variable "Was the advertised unit available to the tester?" the gross incidence of adverse treatment was 17.2, 15.5, 11.1, and 9.5 percentage points for African American-white rental, Hispanic-white rental, African American-white sales, and Hispanic-white sales tests, respectively. The corresponding net incidence of adverse treatment for these samples was 5.5, 8.4, 5.5, and 4.2 percentage points. (See Yinger, 1995, for an in-depth look at the results of the 1989 HDS.) The study also examined geographic differences in treatment for the five in-depth sites and provided estimates of racial steering by neighborhood racial composition, per capita income, and median house value (see Turner and Mikelsons, 1991, for these results).

Other Applications

The first systematic application of paired testing to hiring, conducted in 1989, focused on discrimination against Hispanic men applying for entry-level jobs in Chicago and San Diego. In each of these sites, approximately 150 paired tests were conducted, based on random samples of job openings advertised in the major metropolitan newspapers. A similar study of hiring discrimination against African American men was conducted a year later in Chicago and Washington, D.C. Again, about 200 paired tests were conducted in each metro area, based on random samples of advertised job openings. Both studies found that white applicants were able to advance further in the hiring process than their minority counterparts in a statistically significant share of cases. Specifically, in the Hispanic-white tests in which both testers were able to submit an application, whites received an interview and Hispanics did not 22 percent of the time, while in the African American-white tests, only whites received an interview 9 percent of the time. These numbers are based on the gross measure of adverse treatment. Net adverse treatment was 14 and 6 percent for Hispanic-white and African American-white tests, respectively. In addition, whites were significantly more likely to receive encouragement in the hiring process (Kenney and Wissoker, 1994).

A 1998 pilot study used paired testing to assess the extent and forms of possible discrimination in the home insurance market. Testers in three metropolitan areas posed as buyers of closely matched homes located in minority and white neighborhoods. They called insurance agents on the telephone to seek insurance quotes. The homes, neighborhoods, and insurance seekers were matched on a wide range of characteristics so that the primary difference within a paired test was whether the home was located in a minority or white neighborhood. Results indicated that buyers in white neighborhoods were no more likely than those in minority neighborhoods to receive quotes, but they were slightly more likely to be offered some desirable types of coverage (in one site) and to receive higher levels of service than minorities (in another site). In Phoenix, substantially higher premiums were quoted for homes in Hispanic neighborhoods, but because the white and Hispanic neighborhoods were in different insurance rating territories, the study could not determine definitively whether the difference in premiums might have been due to legitimate differences in rates of risk and loss (Wissoker et al., 1998).

The 1999 Homeownership Testing Project is a pilot study of discrimination in the pre-application phase of the mortgage market. This testing effort includes tests for African Americans and Hispanics in two major metropolitan areas. In each area, a stratified sample of lenders was selected by loan volume based on Home Mortgage Disclosure Act data. The testers were assigned income, assets, and debts sufficient to qualify to purchase a home priced at the median sales price in the area. The assignment was structured so that the qualifying price was constrained by the down payment, and income and debts were assigned so that the mortgage would conform to standard secondary market guidelines. The testers were also provided with an A– credit history profile. The results of this study are not yet available.

In 1999, the Urban Institute analyzed enforcement tests that had been conducted by the National Fair Housing Alliance (NFHA) in five sites. In two of the sites, statistically significant differences were found between the treatment of white and African American testers. White applicants received a quote, defined as information about a loan product with an estimate of monthly mortgage payments and closing costs; African American applicants did not receive a quote in 16 percent of the tests in Chicago and 25 percent of the tests in Atlanta. The net measures of adverse treatment in Chicago and Atlanta were 13 and 25 percent, respectively. It should be noted that the lender sample for the NFHA tests was not random; rather, lenders were chosen using indicators based on the Home Mortgage Disclosure Act data (Smith and Delair, 1999).

2000 HOUSING DISCRIMINATION STUDY: PHASE I

Basic Structure of Study

Phase I of the 2000 HDS is designed to study discrimination in both rental and sales housing markets against African Americans, Hispanics, Asian Americans, and Native Americans. The study will provide estimates of the national incidence and severity of discrimination against African Americans and Hispanics in medium-sized and large metropolitan area housing markets. The study will also provide less precise metropolitan-level estimates of discrimination for all African American and Hispanic sites, as well as metropolitan-level estimates for the pilot Asian American and Native American sites. In the Asian American pilot study, separate estimates will be developed on the basis of different major ethnic subgroups to assess the importance of ethnicity in the treatment of Asian Americans. Finally, given the concentration of the Native American population in small metropolitan and rural areas, the study will include pilot testing for Native Americans in two small metropolitan areas and the surrounding hinterland.

The 2000 HDS follows the basic methodology of the 1989 HDS. The point of entry to the market is an advertisement in a major metropolitan newspaper. The study is based on a sampling of advertisements in the relevant major metropolitan newspapers, followed by a test in which the testers approach the relevant agent or agency and identify their interest in the advertised unit and similar units. The tests are paired in the sense that two individuals, one white and one minority, pose as otherwise identical home seekers. Observed racial differences in treatment between racial groups are interpreted as the adverse treatment expected to be experienced by a qualified minority member inquiring about a randomly chosen housing unit advertised in the newspaper.

The use of a sample of newspaper advertisements offers several advantages. First, the classified advertisements provide a clearly defined list of housing units that are currently on the market and for which information is available to individuals in search of housing. Newspaper advertisements provide a credible starting point for each test. This common starting point increases the match between the two testers' visits relative to simply approaching a real estate agency and therefore increases the statistical power available from a given-sized sample of tests. Finally, the advertisement sampling approach matches the sampling methodology of the 1989 HDS, increasing comparability between the two studies. The weaknesses of the advertisement sampling frame are discussed later in this section.

Sampling Design

The national samples of African American-white and Hispanic-white tests are two-stage samples. First, a sample of sites (16 African American-white and 10 Hispanic-white) is selected from the population of medium-sized to large metropolitan areas with substantial populations of the minority group being tested. A site is included in the sample if the central city population exceeds 100,000 and the percentage of the minority group in the site exceeds that in the U.S. population overall. Probabilities of selection from the population of sites are based on the metropolitan area population. Then, advertisements are drawn weekly from the major metropolitan newspaper in each site. The samples of Asian American and Native American tests are single-stage samples drawn weekly from the major newspapers of individual metropolitan areas (two Asian American sites with three ethnic groups and one Native American site). In all sites, sufficient tests are being conducted to provide metropolitan-level estimates of adverse treatment (72 tests per tenure).

The sampling of advertisements is a centralized process conducted at the Urban Institute in Washington, D.C. The real estate sections of the Sunday newspapers for all sites are shipped to the Urban Institute every Sunday. A site must be sampled within a couple of hours of receipt so the sample can be relayed back to the local fair housing group for testing in a timely fashion. For each site, the order of the advertisement sample is randomized, and the advertisements are forwarded to the local group one at a time (see the next subsection for a more detailed discussion).

One of two sampling methods is used to select advertisements for rental and sales tests—systematic sampling or grid sampling. Systematic sampling involves the "numbering" of advertisements in a newspaper and the subsequent selection of a systematic sample using an interval designed to yield the target number of selections. Systematic sampling is employed when the number of advertisements is relatively small (say, less than 1,000) and confined to a specific format in the classified section. All rental advertisement selections are made using this method. Grid sampling is essentially an area sampling technique whereby a randomly assigned sampling grid is overlaid on the newspaper to reveal the areas (rectangles) that represent the sample. (Application of one grid is tantamount to a 1 in 24 sampling fraction.) Each advertisement is defined by a single point on the newspaper using an objective rule (i.e., the upper corner of the first letter of the first word in the line of descriptive text). Accordingly, all advertisements have the same chance of selection regardless of their size. Grid sampling is used for very large newspaper classified sections that include one or more supplements and can contain up to 3000 advertisements.

Regardless of the selection method, once an advertisement has been selected, it is reviewed to determine eligibility. To be eligible, a housing unit must be within the metropolitan area boundaries, and must be a rental property in a complex represented by an agent or a single-family home or condominium for sale. For example, the rental tests exclude shared rentals, seasonal rentals, and properties rented by owners, while sales tests exclude seasonal or temporary housing, income-generating properties, and properties for sale by the owner. Finally, the advertisement itself may not clearly identify whether a housing unit is eligible so that the eligibility criteria are applied by the local testing agency on the basis of information gathered on site. The sampling team at the Urban Institute draws substantially more advertisements than the number of tests planned in case some are determined to be ineligible by local testing agencies.

At the analysis stage, sample weights will be developed for each ethnic group at both the metropolitan and national levels for the African American-white and Hispanic-white tests. The national sampling weights will be the product of the site selection probability and the probability of selection of the advertisement. This weight will be adjusted for nonresponse to form a national analytic weight for use in national analyses (trends since 1989, as well as year 2000 estimates).

Separate metropolitan analytic weights are being developed for each site. These will be used in creating metropolitan report cards (i.e., developing metro-specific estimates). The metropolitan analytic weight is the product of a sampling weight and a nonresponse adjustment. The sampling weight reflects the probability of selection of the advertisement and incorporates selection within the classified section as well as across weeks. In addition, the sampling weight controls for market saturation within a week if it occurs. In other words, in some small markets or during a week when many advertisements are ineligible, the entire pool of advertisements sent to the local office at a site may be used. Finally, the weights will be adjusted for nonresponse.

To generate confidence intervals, statistical analysis will be conducted for the gross measures and hypothesis tests for the net measures using the sample weights. The standard errors of estimates will be adjusted to account for the complex sampling design; see Kish (1965) and Wolter (1985). Given the small number of tests available in any given test site, statistical analysis will also be conducted for the metropolitan report cards using exact permutation tests (see Agresti, 1990, for a general discussion and Heckman and Siegelman, 1993, for the use of these tests in a testing context).

Test Protocol

A test begins with the selection of an eligible advertisement at the Urban Institute and the submission of a test authorization form to the local test coordinator specifying the type of test to be conducted, the order in which the testers should contact the housing provider, and whether a narrative (a quality control measure) must be completed for this test. Selection proceeds in order of the randomized list of advertisements An advance call by a nonminority individual to obtain information concerning availability (rental tests only), price, size, and location is conducted for all rental tests and for sales tests if this information is not available in the advertisement. Tester income and financial characteristics (sales tests only) are assigned to match the price of the housing unit. Occupations and employers are assigned consistent with these characteristics, but specific occupations (e.g., law enforcement) and regional employers are excluded based on the belief that these occupations or employers might receive some special treatment. Marital status and family structure are assigned on the basis of the size of the unit and the desire to obtain a fairly equal distribution of family types.

The local agency assigns the selected advertisement to one minority and one white tester as soon as two testers of the same gender and comparable ages are available. The testers each call to set up an appointment and visit in alternating order. These calls should be 1 to 6 hours apart for rental testing and 24 to 48 hours apart for sales testing. The actual tester visits should also be 1 to 6 hours apart for rental testing and 24 to 96 hours apart for sales testing. Rental testers make one visit to a rental housing site to inquire about the availability of the advertised and similar units. A similar protocol is followed by sales testers, except that the tester is available for a follow-up visit to see additional units, and provision has been made to record follow-up phone calls by the real estate agent. Testers are required to take notes during their visit and to document its results on standardized forms within 1 hour of completing the visit. The local test coordinator debriefs all testers, and also collects and reviews all test file materials. Test narratives are required on a small number of randomly chosen tests to provide information for a quality control review of test files. Testers are not informed that a narrative is required prior to performing the test.

Limitations of and Alternatives to
Random Sampling of Advertisements

While the use of a sample of advertisements offers many advantages, there are a number of disadvantages associated with this sampling strategy. First, the units advertised in the newspaper may not accurately represent the population of available housing units. Units may be advertised because they are especially attractive or in desirable neighborhoods and will attract clients to the agency. Alternatively, some units may not be advertised to more closely control the population of home seekers who have access to a unit or the neighborhood in which it is located. Moreover, in the case of sales tests, most home buyers do not learn from the newspaper about the home they actually purchase. Finally, the importance of newspapers in marketing housing may be declining in significance over time as the Internet is increasingly used to market a wide variety of products.

Within Phase I of HDS 2000, a two-pronged strategy is being used to examine the limitations of the newspaper sampling frame, to be carried out in a small number of pilot sites. First, newspapers list housing advertisements by community and sometimes by smaller geographic regions for large central cities. The distribution of advertisements by community will be examined and compared with estimates of the distribution of rental and owner-occupied housing across communities in each of the pilot sites. This comparison will make it possible to identify communities in which housing units are underrepresented in newspaper advertisements and to draw additional samples of advertisements from these communities.

Second, after the completion of a test, the actual address of the advertised unit is available. The Urban Institute will perform a geographic analysis of these addresses in an attempt to identify regions of the metropolitan area that do not appear in the sample of advertisements, and will acquire socioeconomic characteristics for regions and/or neighborhoods from private vendors, such as Claritas. Once these regions have been identified, six to ten neighborhoods (three to five per tenure) will be selected, and a variety of local or neighborhood-level sources will be used to identify housing units for testing. These tests will be used for comparison with traditional advertisement-based tests, but cannot be combined with the sample of the latter because of the nonrandom nature of the selection process.

There are many other types of marketing that might be considered for Phases II and III of HDS 2000. First, the population of advertisements might be expanded to include Internet and other easily observable metropolitan-wide sources of advertisements. This expansion would likely increase the base of marketed units covered without sacrificing comparability to Phase I because the sample would still be drawn from a metropolitan-wide sample of advertisements. The addition of local sources of advertisements (below the metropolitan level) as discussed above would expand the base further, but at the expense of comparability. Other, more extreme modifications to the protocols might involve a sampling of agencies and agents rather than advertisements. As discussed earlier, it can be quite difficult to compile a complete, nonduplicative list of rental or sales real estate agents, and nearly impossible to obtain any measure of volume for these agents. Finally, attempts might be made to sample available units. One possibility is the random sampling of streets and the second-stage selection of street-level advertisements from the selected streets. This approach might provide a fairly representative sample of units for sales tests (with the exception of condominiums), but is unlikely to provide a representative sample for rental tests since the use of street-level advertisements for rental properties is far less uniform.

Imperfect Pairs and Differences Across Visits

As discussed earlier, the paired-testing approach is unlikely to yield a perfect match within a test. First, the testers approach the selected agent at different times, and as a result the circumstances and treatment they encounter may differ. The possibility of such differences implies that the frequency of adverse treatment of minority testers, the gross measure, may capture differences that do not represent discrimination. In addition, testers are paired only on gender and age, and therefore may differ on many characteristics that might influence behavior during a test. This second problem may exacerbate the error in gross adverse treatment as a measure of discrimination while creating the potential for more severe biases in the analysis. Specifically, the populations of white and minority testers may differ systematically on characteristics that influence treatment. If so, the net and gross measures capture a combination of discrimination and the effect of racial differences in unobserved tester characteristics.

The 2000 HDS is attempting to address these issues. To the author's knowledge, Phase I of this study is the first paired-testing effort that records actual tester characteristics and makes those characteristics available for analysis. The characteristics collected include employment status and history, education level, individual and household income, household structure, and experience as a home seeker. Earlier research by Heckman and Siegelman (1993) and Ondrich et al. (2000, 2001) found only limited evidence that tester characteristics affect treatment. The data analyzed in these studies, however, contain no information about testers beyond an identification number, and these analyses were based on examining the experiences of pairs of testers who conducted multiple tests together. In HDS 2000, the analysis will exploit the information on actual tester characteristics, as well as test characteristics such as the attributes of the advertised unit and observed circumstances during a tester's visit, to determine whether these factors influence treatment and whether such influences affect observed net and gross adverse treatment.

Finally, Phase II of the 2000 HDS will include three-person or triplet tests to examine the influence of random differences between visits and testers on observed adverse treatment. These tests will take two forms: minority-white-white and white-minority-minority. The form will be randomized over tests. This approach will minimize noise by limiting the time between same-race visits while also ensuring that the first two visits of each triplet will yield a standard paired test.

REFERENCES

Agresti, Alan
  1990 *Categorical Data Analysis.* New York: John Wiley and Sons.
Fix, M., G. Galster, and R. Struyk
  1993 An overview of auditing for discrimination. In *Clear and Convincing Evidence: Testing for Discrimination in America,* M. Fix and R. Struyk, eds. Washington, D.C.: Urban Institute Press.
Heckman, J., and P. Siegelman
  1993 The Urban Institute studies: Their methods and findings. In *Clear and Convincing Evidence: Testing for Discrimination in America,* M. Fix and R. Struyk, eds. Washington, D.C.: Urban Institute Press.
Kenney, G.M., and D.A. Wissoker
  1994 An analysis of the correlates of discrimination facing young Hispanic job-seekers. *American Economic Review* 84(June):674-683.
Kish, L.
  1965 *Survey Sampling.* New York: John Wiley and Sons.
Ondrich, J., S. Ross, and J. Yinger
  2001 Now You See It, Now You Don't: Why Some Homes Are Hidden From Black Buyers. Unpublished manuscript.
Ondrich, J., S. Ross, and J. Yinger
  2000 How common is housing discrimination? Improving on traditional measures. *Journal of Urban Economics* (47):470-500.
Ross, S., and J. Yinger
  1999 Does discrimination exist? The Boston Fed study and its critics. In *Mortgage Lending Discrimination: A Review of Existing Evidence,* M. Turner and F. Skidmore, eds. Urban Institute Monograph Series on Race and Discrimination. Washington, DC: Urban Institute Press.
Smith, R., and M. Delair
  1999 New evidence from lender testing: Discrimination at the pre-application stage. In *Mortgage Lending Discrimination: A Review of Existing Evidence,* M. Turner and F. Skidmore, eds. Urban Institute Monograph Series on Race and Discrimination. Washington, DC: Urban Institute Press.
Turner, M.A., and M. Mikelsons
  1991 Patterns of racial steering in four metropolitan areas. *Journal of Housing Economics* (2):199-234.
Wissoker, D., W. Zimmermann, and G. Galster
  1998 *Testing for Discrimination in Home Insurance.* Washington, D.C.: Urban Institute Press.
Wolter, K.
  1985 *Introduction to Variance Estimation.* New York: Springer-Verlag, Inc.
Yinger, J.
  1995 *Closed Doors, Opportunities Lost: The Continuing Costs of Housing Discrimination.* New York: Russell Sage Foundation.

Appendix B

Audit Studies and the Assessment of Discrimination

S.A. Murphy

The Housing Discrimination Study (HDS) uses primarily audit studies to estimate *overall-level discrimination* against ethnic/racial groups. Overall-level discrimination occurs when there is ethnic/racial discrimination averaged across realtors, applicants (i.e., auditors), and circumstances. By realtor is meant housing realtors and other purveyors of housing; by circumstances is meant the circumstances of the contact between the auditor and the realtor. Overall-level discrimination is of course different from *individual-level discrimination,* in which particular auditors are discriminated against because of ethnic status. To simplify the following discussion, the term "black" is used to encompass racial minorities.

Discrimination here refers to *adverse market discrimination,* which can occur in two ways. Discrimination against blacks occurs when race = black is a direct reason for the realtor to produce a negative outcome *or* when race = black is used by the realtor as a surrogate for unobserved measures of (renter/buyer) suitability that vary in distribution across the racial groups. The former is direct discrimination, and the latter is statistical discrimination.

Realtors should strive to ascertain all qualification measures directly, including those that vary in distribution across racial groups. Realtors are

S.A. Murphy works for the Department of Statistics and Institute for Social Research at the University of Michigan.

not to use race as a surrogate for qualification measures. More work is needed to assist well-intentioned realtors (with an imperfect ability to assess qualifications) in avoiding the use of race as a surrogate for qualifications.

Since individual-level discrimination and overall-level discrimination are easily confused when discussing the utility of the audit model, the two are discussed in turn below.

THE AUDIT MODEL AND INDIVIDUAL-LEVEL DISCRIMINATION

Sometimes audit results are reported by audit pair (averaged over realtors and circumstances of audit visits). Audit results reported for a particular pair may be misconstrued as estimates of net or gross individual-level discrimination. However, even under extremely optimal conditions, audit results for a particular pair cannot be interpreted as estimates of individual-level discrimination. Suppose the audit coordinator is successful in matching the audit pair on all possible qualifications (that vary in distribution by race). One can expect there to be many individual characteristics that do not vary across the two racial groups (black/white), yet are used in assessing renter qualifications. These characteristics may or may not be truly indicative of one's qualifications. Moreover, since the characteristics are equivalently distributed across racial groups, their use does not constitute discrimination between racial groups. The individuals in the audit pair may not be equal on these characteristics; thus the realtor may treat the individuals in the audit pair unequally, yet no discrimination occurs. Fallibility in assessing qualifications may lead to this situation. To emphasize this observation more strongly, even if both of the members of the audit are white, it may be expected that audit results for one pair (averaged over realtors and circumstances of audit visits) would result in nonzero "estimates" of individual-level measures of discrimination.

The conclusion is that audit results presented by audit pair do not represent individual-level discrimination unless an extremely strong assumption holds. This assumption is that the auditors are matched on all qualifications and individual characteristics regardless of whether these qualifications/characteristics vary by race. This assumption appears impractical and unnecessary when the goal is to ascertain overall-level discrimination. It is difficult to see how this level of matching can be achieved in practice. Indeed, this level of matching (i.e., the test coordinator has matched the members of the pair not only on all possible qualifications that vary in distribution by race, but also on all possible individual characteristics that vary in distribution by race) will not hold even in optimal settings. The economic agent may treat the members of the audit pair differently because of differing individual characteristics that do not vary by race. Of course, if the audit results for one audit pair are extremely gross, one may be inclined to believe that there are no individual characteristics/qualifications that could have produced such a gross effect.

THE AUDIT MODEL AND OVERALL-LEVEL DISCRIMINATION

As long as audit pairs are matched on all qualifications that vary in distribution by race, audit results averaged over realtors, circumstances of the visits, and auditors can be viewed as an unbiased estimate of overall-level discrimination (i.e., average level of adverse market discrimination). This is because one averages overall individual auditor characteristics (as opposed to the case of individual-level discrimination, in which audit results are to be averaged only over realtors and circumstances of the visits).

The following is a quantitative explanation in which:

f is used to denote densities.

e is race (black/white).

ea is realtor (realty, etc.).

$r(ea)$ is the realtor's legitimate applicant requirements/qualifications that vary in distribution by race (income requirements, credit requirements, etc.).

ic is individual auditor characteristics that do not vary in distribution by race. That is, $f(ic|e) = f(ic)$.

ice is individual auditor characteristics that may vary in distribution by race and are not in $r(ea)$. That is, $f(ice|e,r(ea),ic)$ is not identically equal to $f(ice|r(ea),ic)$. There is a dependence of f on $r(ea)$ since applicant requirements may vary by realtor, and thus $r(ea)$ may include more or less of the set of all individual auditor characteristics varying by race.

c is circumstances of the audit visit unconnected with the particular individual auditor (e.g., the apartment was rented in the meantime).

X is 1 if the realtor says the advertised apartment is available, 0 otherwise. X is indexed by all factors that contribute to a result of 1 or 0. X is an unknown nonparametric function: $X(e,r(ea),ice, ic,ea,c)$.

Technically, $X = X(e,r(ea),ice,ic,ea,c)$ may be viewed as a nonparametric structural equation in the terminology of Pearl (2000).

Suppose the audit pair is composed of one white and one black. The two individuals are assigned the same realtor (same *ea*) and are assigned or possess the same values as the realtor's legitimate requirements, $r(ea)$. They have different individual characteristics, denoted by *(ice′, ic′)* and *(ice″, ic″)*, respectively. Also, since they must visit the agent at different times, the circumstances will be different as well (*c′* and *c″*).

The net average or overall-level discrimination estimate is then found by averaging

$$X(e = w, r(ea),ice′,ic′,ea,c′) - X(e = b,r(ea),ice″,ic″,ea,c″)$$

over circumstances, realtors, and audit pairs. This results in an estimator for

$$\int (X(w,r(ea),ice,ic,ea,c) \ f(ice|w,r(ea),ic) \tag{1}$$
$$-X(b,r(ea),ice,ic,ea,c) \ f(ice|b, r(ea),ic)) \ \ f(c,ea) \ f(ic) \ d(ea,c,ice,ic),$$

where $f(c,ea)$ is determined by the selection of advertisements and the visit times of the auditors (this density is the same for both members of the audit pair since they ask about the same advertisement, and the order of the visits is randomized); where $f(ic)$ is determined by the selection of the auditors; and where $f(ice|w,r(ea),ic)$ is determined by the realtor's suitability requirements and the selection of the auditors. In addition, $f(ice|w,r(ea),ic) \neq f(ice|b,r(ea),ic)$ since there are individual characteristics that vary in distribution between the racial groups.

The above difference is zero if $X(e,r(ea),ice,ic,ea,c)$ is constant in both *e* and *ice*, that is, if the realtor's judgment of suitability does not directly employ race or employ race as a surrogate for individual characteristics (not in *r(ea)*) that vary in distribution by race. This is exactly what would be expected from a measure of overall discrimination.

COMMENTS

Audit pairs need only be matched on all qualifications that vary in distribution by race to provide an unbiased estimate of average or overall discrimination. Audit pairs may be matched on other characteristics (to improve statistical power), but this is not necessary to produce an unbiased estimator of net average or overall discrimination. Moreover, to accumulate information about discrimination, one needs many audit pairs. Multiple audits by audit pairs can be used to hold costs down, but one does not thereby accumulate information about discrimination. Information about discrimination is not accumulated because the members of the audit pair may differ in *ic*, individual characteristics that are distributed equally in the two races. Differential treatment of the members of the auditor pair due to *ic* is not adverse discrimination.

Improving the Matching on All Qualifications that Vary in Distribution by Race

Estimation of net overall discrimination requires that the audit pair be matched on all suitability qualifications that vary in distribution by race. It can be expected that these qualifications will vary by economic agent. Furthermore, it is unrealistic to expect the HDS to be aware of all of realtors' suitability qualifications. The HDS can assign qualifications to an audit pair in a way that depends on the realtors. First, the customary qualifications/requirements (such as creditworthiness, income, and employer/occupation) are assigned. Then, after audit pairs have been randomized to realtors and individuals within the audit pair randomized by order, the first auditor should record all questions asked and answers given that are not part of the assigned customary requirements. The test coordinator can then use the additional information requested of the first auditor to form a closer match by maintaining a consistent life story for the second auditor. Thus the realtor determines which individual characteristics (beyond the customary suitability requirements and race) will be matched.

Determining Whether the Overall Discrimination Effect Is a "Market-Level" Discrimination Effect

It is of low utility to discover that agents handling homes for which most blacks could not reasonably qualify are discriminatory. It is much more useful to discover that agents handling homes well within the reach of many blacks are discriminatory.

It appears that the distribution of the prices of the homes used in the HDS should match the distribution of creditworthiness, income, and employer/occupation among blacks rather than an overall average distribution of creditworthiness, income, and employer/occupation. This point is in line with the idea that it is important to ascertain discrimination in situations in which blacks are qualified buyers. This is not the same as saying that the impact of discrimination is most important at the realties blacks choose to use, but that the impact of discrimination is most important at the realties that sell homes blacks are qualified to buy.

The above point can be seen from display (1), in which the differences

$$(X(w,r(ea),ice,ic,ea,c) \, f(ice|w,r(ea),ic) -$$
$$X(b,r(ea),ice,ic,ea,c) \, f(ice|b,r(ea),ic))$$

are weighed by the density *f(c,ea)*. Thus large differences can be paired with a small *f(c,ea)* weight and vice versa, and so the definition of overall-level discrimination changes with the distribution of realtors, *ea*.

How difficult would it be to match the market to the qualifications of blacks; that is, to choose home advertisements (i.e., realtors) with probabilities proportional to the "appropriate" segment of the black population?

REFERENCE

Pearl, J.
   2000   *Causality: Models, Reasoning, and Inference.* New York: Cambridge University Press.

Appendix C

Workshop Materials

Workshop on the Measurement of Discrimination in Housing
Washington, DC
September 22-23, 2000

AGENDA

Friday, September 22, 2000

8:30 am   Continental Breakfast

9:00   Welcome and Opening Remarks
Stephen Fienberg, Workshop Chair
Faith Mitchell, Director, Division on Social and Economic Studies
Andy White, Director, Committee on National Statistics

9:15   Introduction of Workshop Presenters and Participants

Part I: The 1989 and 2000 HDS Audits

9:30   Purpose of the HUD Housing Discrimination Study (HDS) Audit
Todd Richardson and David Chase, U.S. Department of Housing and Urban Development

Discussion

10:00   Phase I of the 2000 HDS Audit
               Margery Turner and Rob Santos, The Urban Institute

               Discussion

11:00   Break

11:15   Key Policy and Methodological Issues Related to the Urban
               Institute Study
               *Discussants: Gregory Squires, Arthur Goldberger, Stephen
                   Fienberg*

               General Discussion

12:15 pm   Lunch (continuation of discussion, if needed)

Part II: Preparing for Phase II of the HDS Audit

1:00   Auditing Discrimination in "Underserved" Urban
               Communities
               Issues Involved: *Margery Turner and Rob Santos*
               Discussants: Nancy Denton, Lawrence Bobo, Min Zhou

               General Discussion

3:00   Break

3:15   Implications of the Methodological Discussion for the Phase
               II Design Plan
               Discussants: Tom Louis, Sanders Korenman

               General Discussion

4:30   Wrap-up
               Stephen Fienberg

5:00   Adjourn

Saturday, September 23, 2000

Part III: The Methodology of Measuring Discrimination

8:30 am   Continental Breakfast

9:00   Challenges Raised by Heterogeneity and Paired Testing
             Discussants: Joseph Altonji, Arthur Goldberger

             General Discussion

10:00   Derivation, Presentation, and Interpretation of National
             Estimates
             Discussant: Thomas Jabine

             General Discussion

11:00   Break

11:15   Implications of the Discussion for Other Research; Alternate
             Methodologies
             Discussants: Charles Manski, Susan Murphy

             General Discussion

12:15pm   Lunch (continuation of discussion)

12:45   Wrap-up
             Stephen Fienberg

             Discussion

1:30   Adjourn

PARTICIPANTS

Stephen Fienberg (*Chair*), Center for Automated Learning and Discovery, Carnegie Mellon University

Joseph Altonji, Department of Economics, Northwestern University

Lawrence Bobo, Department of Sociology, Harvard University

Amy Bogdon, Fannie Mae Foundation

David Chase, U.S. Department of Housing and Urban Development

Nancy Denton, State University of New York, Albany

Brian Doherty, U.S. Department of Housing and Urban Development

Julie Fernandes, Civil Rights Division, U.S. Department of Justice

Angela Williams Foster, The H. John Heinz School of Public Policy and Management, Carnegie Mellon University

Arthur Goldberger, Department of Economics, University of Wisconsin

Bryan Greene, U.S. Department of Housing and Urban Development

Thomas Jabine, Committee on National Statistics, National Research Council

Sanders Korenman, Center for the Study of Business and Government, Baruch College, City University of New York

Thomas Louis, The RAND Corporation

Charles Manski, Department of Economics, Northwestern University

Joan A. Magagna, Housing and Civil Enforcement Section, U.S. Department of Justice

Myrna McKinnon, Division on Social and Economic Studies, National Research Council

Faith Mitchell, Division on Social and Economic Studies, National Research Council

Susan Murphy, Statistics Department and Survey Research Center, University of Michigan

Kevin Neary, U.S. Department of Housing and Urban Development

Harriett Newburger, U.S. Department of Housing and Urban Development

Leonard J. Norry, U.S. Bureau of the Census

Susan Offutt, Economic Research, U.S. Department of Agriculture

Kris Rengert, Fannie Mae Foundation

Todd Richardson, U.S. Department of Housing and Urban Development

Stephen Ross, Department of Economics, University of Connecticut

Rob Santos, The Urban Institute

Ashish Sen, Bureau of Transportation Statistics, U.S. Department of
    Transportation
Mark Shroder, U.S. Department of Housing and Urban Development
Patrick Simmons, Fannie Mae Foundation
Roberta Spalter-Roth, Research Program on the Discipline and the
    Profession, American Sociological Association
Gregory Squires, Department of Sociology, The George Washington
    University
Margery Turner, The Urban Institute
Amy L. Wax, University of Virginia School of Law
Katherine Wallman, Office of Information and Regulatory Affairs, U.S.
    Office of Management and Budget
Andy White, Committee on National Statistics, National Research
    Council
Cathy Spatz Widom, Department of Psychiatry, New Jersey Medical
    School
Min Zhou, Office of Educational Research and Improvement, U.S.
    Department of Education